AF263977

FALLING TO FLY

THE BOOK TO READ BEFORE YOU
GIVE UP ON YOUR WRITING DREAMS

Todd Fahnestock

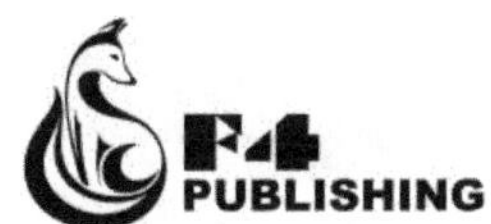

ISBN 978-1-952699-58-0

Cover design by:
Todd Fahnestock & Quincy J. Allen

Dedication

To the *Falling to Fly* Fellowship
Thank you for the Zoom call. It made all the difference.

CONTENTS

FALLING TO FLY

Chapter 1 – The Nightmare	1
Chapter 2 – The Dream	7
Chapter 3 – Demons	16
Chapter 4 – Selective Ignorance	23
Chapter 5 – The Little Rebel	27
Chapter 6 – Dancing with the Universe	37
Chapter 7 – Trusting the Voice	45
Chapter 8 – Writing from the Heart	53
Chapter 9 – The Hunt for Magic	57
Chapter 10 – New York	64
Chapter 11 – The Agent	67
Chapter 12 – Cold Product	74
Chapter 13 – Confidence	77
Chapter 14 – Rising Again	81
Chapter 15 – Commitment	91
Chapter 16 – The Jump	100
Chapter 17 – Goodbye to Trad Publishing	105
Chapter 18 – Indie Author	109
Chapter 19 – Say Yes to Everything	113

Chapter 20 – Salesman 116

Chapter 21 – Rapid Release 121

Chapter 22 – The Two Journeys 126

Chapter 23 – Writer's Adrenaline 129

Chapter 24 – The Muse 133

Chapter 25 – Aligning for Success 139

Chapter 26 – The Good Reviews 141

Chapter 27 – Beginner's Mind 146

Chapter 28 – Leveling Up 150

Chapter 29 – Flying 155

Mailing List/Social Media

MAILING LIST
Don't miss out on the latest news and information about all of
my books. Join my Readers Group:
https://www.subscribepage.com/u0x4q3

FACEBOOK
https://www.facebook.com/todd.fahnestock

AMAZON AUTHOR PAGE
https://www.amazon.com/Todd-
Fahnestock/e/B004N1MILG

FALLING TO FLY

THE BOOK TO READ BEFORE YOU GIVE UP ON YOUR WRITING DREAMS

1

THE NIGHTMARE

MY WRITING CAREER BEGAN WITH A NIGHTMARE.

When I was young, just about the time the arguments between my parents were growing more and more heated, I began to have a recurring dream.

I stood on a promontory that stuck out from a sheer mountain like the prow of a ship, except there were no guardrails. I appeared in the dream with my hands out like a tightrope walker, looking over the breathtaking drop, the distant mountains, and a single house on the ground far below, so far below that it could have been a satellite snapshot.

My heart raced, and I fought the vertigo. I didn't know how I'd come to be on the cliff; all I knew was that I needed to get the hell away from that edge as fast as I could. The ground of the promontory was flat, and there was no wind, but it felt like I was being drawn toward the edge.

I backed away, feeling better with every step. One step… One more… And one more… My racing heart began to calm with each inch I retreated.

I bumped into something.

My gaze had been fixed on the tip of that promontory and the empty expanse of air. I hadn't been looking where I was going, and when I turned, I came face to face with—

Nothing.

In front of me was the ever-thickening base of the promontory. A short distance away, it connected to the mountain and a friendly looking path continued both ways along the edge. Safety. Security.

But I couldn't get to it. There was some kind of invisible wall in front of me. I was blocked.

I pushed at it. Nothing. I beat my fists on it. Nothing. I started to move toward the edge, to see if there was a gap—

The invisible wall started moving toward me, pushing me away from the safety of the mountainside, pushing me toward the drop.

"No!" I shouted at the thing and redoubled my efforts, pounding with my fists, but it was as solid as stone. It didn't shimmy, shudder, or budge in the slightest.

Terror coursed over me like icy water as I flipped around and put my back against it, feet scrabbling on the sandstone as it pushed me inexorably toward the edge.

Fifteen feet… Ten feet… Five feet…

All I could hear was the painful thumping of my heart as I reached the point where I'd appeared at the beginning of the dream. I scrabbled harder, feet sliding, shouting.

Mercilessly, the invisible wall pushed me over the edge.

I fell, screaming and screaming, falling so long that my ragged throat hurt as the ground rushed up at me and—

I awoke, sitting up in bed, breathing hard.

In the following days, though I didn't tell anyone about my dream, I asked about dreams, about falling dreams in specific. I didn't ask my parents, but instead my junior high school friends.

I heard lots of stories, but the one that stuck with me was this: if you hit the ground in a falling dream while you're asleep, you die in real life.

Junior high wisdom.

The dream didn't come to me every night, and it didn't come regularly. I would get a few nights' rest. Sometimes I'd get a few weeks. Never more than a month. And then, at random…

The nightmare would return.

It was always the same.

I appeared on the precipice. I tried to leave. I was blocked by the wall. The wall started moving and pushed me over the edge. I fell and fell and—

I woke up.

The arguments between my parents in real life heightened. I remember my mother losing a lot of money in a business venture. I remember my father yelling at her as she left the house, telling her that if she didn't get back inside, he'd kick her butt right through her teeth.

At night, the nightmare continued. The same every time. In the dream, my chest hurt at the terror, and I'd wake up with it still hurting.

I told no one.

I had other nightmares. Demons would come for me at night, and I'd run away from them. But those dreams changed every time. The falling nightmare was always the same.

Things progressed with my parents, and they separated. My father moved away to California. We stayed in Colorado. I progressed through junior high and into high school.

During my sophomore year, when we were living in one of the string of shabbier and shabbier apartments my mom could afford, the nightmare changed.

Or rather, it's more accurate to say: I changed it.

That night, I appeared a couple feet from the tip of the promontory, just as always.

On many other nights, I had tried everything I could to get past the barrier. I'd sprinted toward it to see if I could get past it before it formed. I'd leapt high to see if there was a way I could get over it. I'd tried to sneak around the edge to see if I could circumvent it.

Nothing had worked.

In the wake of my parent's divorce, though, something had broken inside me. I was still terrified of the wall, still terrified of the fall, but I was also angry now. I hated how my happy little life had been blown apart. I hated how my parents couldn't keep things together. I hated how, up until this moment, I'd thought they knew everything about everything. I realized now that they didn't, that they were just as confused and fucked up as everyone else.

Most of all, I hated the futility of this nightmare. No matter what I did, I couldn't escape it. There was no safety here.

I strode to the wall, put my hands on it, felt the cool, hard nothingness against my cheek. It began its inevitable push that, in about fifteen seconds, was going to dump me over the edge.

I shoved away, spun in mid-step, and sprinted toward the tip of the promontory. I ran as hard as I could, arms pumping at my sides. I couldn't stop the damned wall from shoving me over the edge, but I could sure as hell deny it the pleasure.

I reached edge and I leapt off.

Air rushed past me. I winged my arms spastically, and I screamed—part terror, part rage. I couldn't stop from falling… I was going to hit again, just as before.

Then I heard a voice inside me. It wasn't my voice. Or maybe it was. A voice of some future self, some wiser self. To this day, I don't know where it came from. It said:

If you can just hold yourself together… If you can just hold yourself together… you can fly.

I didn't know what that meant, or how I was supposed to use it to fly, but suddenly it felt like my body wanted to come apart in six pieces. My arms and legs wanted to fly away from my torso. My head wanted to fly off my neck. It felt like I was being pulled apart by the force of the very air.

Screaming through my gritted teeth, I held myself together. The air rushed by me. The ground rushed closer.

And I saw something I hadn't seen before.

A line of tall posts strung power lines one to the next, off into the distance.

The force of my leap had taken me out from the cliff. I was

not falling to the base anymore. I realized with the first flash of hope I'd had since this stupid nightmare had started that I might be able to make it to those power lines.

Thinking that seemed to angle me toward them. I hit them, and like some Looney Tunes character, I hit with my feet, the wire bowed nearly to the ground…

And shot me back up into the air.

I screamed again, but this time with exhilaration. I hadn't hit the ground. I was still falling but… upward.

The arc came to its zenith, inevitably, and I began to fall to the ground again. I felt that sense of being pulled apart.

I held myself together.

And I saw the house, that house I'd seen from so far above, but this time it was at a much more manageable distance. The roof was comparatively huge, and I realized if I could just hit that house, that sloped roof, I might bounce again.

And I did.

My feet hit and I launched. I didn't have the powerful spring of the wire this time, but my leap flung me a good ten feet into the air. Now I was only twenty-five feet from the ground. All I needed was something cushy, something…

A dilapidated old couch hunched at the side of the house, clearly left out in the weather to be taken to the dump.

I landed on it, sprung five feet into the air and…

I landed on the ground.

At first, I simply couldn't believe it. What kind of ridiculous string of unlikely events could have landed me on the ground, but…

Here I was. I was standing on solid earth. I had beaten the invisible wall! I'd beaten that stupid cliff and its stupid promontory.

I looked behind me, saw the thing looming, looking down on me impassively. I shouted at it and gave it a one-finger salute.

I danced around in victory, looking at the cliff, at the power lines, at the house, at the couch, and at the distant mountains. I must have danced like that for five minutes.

And then I awoke. Not with my heart hammering, not with my chest hurting. I awoke with a smile.

The next night, the nightmare came again. I did the same thing. I sprinted. I leapt. Powerlines. House. Couch. Ground.

The next night, it came again, as though to check one final time. I sprinted. I leapt. Powerlines. House. Couch. Ground.

That was the last time I ever had the dream. I never saw that cliff again, except in my memories.

The day after, a new dream started. I began in the wide-open field beyond the cliff. I knew that's where it was, but I never turned around to look at the cliff or the house. The power lines were just behind me, but I was focused on the field and the mountains in the distance. I found that, by exerting my will and angling my hands just-so, I could lift my body up into air. I could fly!

I was free.

The day after that, I began writing my first book, about heroes in a fantasy world, doing the impossible.

To this day, whenever I feel in over my head, whenever it feels like my life is sliding into the toilet, I get that same sensation of my body being pulled apart in those six pieces. I hold them together.

And every time, I've come through the hardship.

This was how writing began for me.

2

THE DREAM

I MENTIONED THE NIGHTMARE. Let's talk about The Dream. This is the tantalizing vision that coalesces and sets a writer on the path. It is that moment of realization that shackles them to this crazy life. For some people, this happens in elementary school when they show their mom their first short story. For some, it can happen when they retire from their first career as a lawyer at age sixty.

Mine happened my senior year in high school.

So many things came together in an amorphous sequence from the moment my parents split. I went from elementary school to junior high to high school somewhere in there. I went from a secure home life to a free fall into the wide-open world, from content to fearful to determined.

My recurring nightmare ran side-by-side with my parent's divorce. The divorce ran side-by-side with my discovery of epic fantasy stories. Those inspiring stories interlaced with blossoming hormones and the other transformations of growing up.

These once-in-a-lifetime elements smashed together and

kicked off my desire to write my own fantasy stories.

I put fingers to keyboard for the first time in my senior year of high school. My writing career sprouted at that moment, but fate planted the seed on a rainy day back in junior high.

My school, Smiley Junior High, was a beige brick building. It looked like Hollywood's interpretation of a mental institution. Which was appropriate, being as this was where they crammed all the hormone-hopped teenagers.

I used to stare out of those tall windows during class, at the green world outside, wishing I was anywhere else and praying that Jack Parker wasn't going to be waiting in the hallway when class was done. He'd threatened to beat me up three days in a row now, and I was certain one of these days he was going to catch me. I always envisioned it happening in one of the deserted concrete stairways, where he'd pound my head into one of the steel-banded steps.

He and his friends had already caught me once in the bathroom, picked me up, and almost shoved my head into a toilet. This was the classic bit of junior high torture called The Swirlie back in the day. They'd only stopped with my head an inch from the water because my best friend at the time had been there, a witness. I'd struggled like a worm on a hook, and they'd laughed. My friend had laughed, too, and maybe that's why they'd stopped. They'd clearly proven their dominance, after all. Why take that small extra step that would land them in the principal's office. I don't know.

So on that day when fate waited patiently for me, I moved quickly down the stairways, two hands on the guard rail so I could peek around the corners as I descended. I slipped through the side door and out onto the street, keeping my head low and my backpack hunched up on my shoulders.

Ironically, Jack and I had been friends back in elementary school. He didn't live far from my house, and we'd often gotten together to play. But during one of those play dates, we'd started a foolish game of knee-riding on a skateboard down a bumpy sidewalk. Knees down, feet behind us, head sticking forward like the prow of a ship, and our center of balance somewhere close to our nose. He hit a mismatched square of concrete, pitched forward face-first, and knocked his two front teeth out. Right clean out.

He hated me from that day forward.

I wasn't the reason he lost his teeth that day, but I was standing right there. I watched the whole thing. Hell, I'd been doing the same stupid thing until I saw what happened to him. When he became my nightmare bully in junior high, that elementary school accident was the only explanation I could think of as to why he hated me so much. I suppose he blamed me for it, somehow.

Regardless, I became the focus of his anger.

And the first five minutes after class were the most dangerous. If he noticed me while he was surrounded by his friends—all of whom seemed inordinately huge—Jack was unstoppable. If he was alone, he'd just glare at me. But if he was with his friends, he'd boast, point at me, and then he'd have to follow through on his threats. So if I could just get free of the math, English, and sciences building—there were two primary buildings that comprised Smiley Junior High—and over to the music, drama, and foreign languages building, I'd be safe.

The buses lined up in the little dogleg street between the two buildings, and most kids hung out there after school. If Jack Parker caught sight of me before I made it past the dogleg—and he was with his friends—there'd be a chase. If he didn't, I'd be safe.

Just beyond the dogleg was the place where the buses lined up, and that was its own little slice of hell. I'd heard there was a group of kids going around with sewing needles scotch taped to the end of plastic Bic pens. They'd sneak behind the lines of people waiting for the bus and randomly stab guys in the ass. This was the latest, freshest terror.

Junior high in the 1980s sucked.

Lucky for me, I didn't have to wait in line for the bus that day. My brother had just turned sixteen and had his own car—

a bright orange 1967 El Camino with a Corvette engine in it. We called it The Great Pumpkin. He was in high school now, but he'd conceded to swing by the junior high after school to take me home.

All I had to do was kill a half an hour, so I wandered over to the library across the street. This was a blessed safe zone. Bullies never hung out at the public library.

Also, I'd discovered a secret that had piqued the interest of this hormone-addled fourteen-year-old boy. The library was packed with books, but it also carried magazines.

Now, normally this wouldn't have mattered at all to me. I wasn't much of a magazine guy. Comic books, yes. Magazines, no. And the library didn't carry comic books at that time (booo!). Instead, it was National Geographic, Newsweek, People, Sports Illustrated, etc. For my part, I had little interest in elephants in Africa or what the president of the United States was doing. I had even less interest in the celebrities of my mom's generation. And I hated sports. I didn't give a crap about what baseball team had traded so-and-so to such-and-such. Sports Illustrated was, like, the worst.

Or, at least, it *had* been…

In my hours at the library, picking through the boring magazines in a desperate attempt to find something—anything—that more closely approximated a Marvel comic book, I discovered a treasure trove. Once a year Sports Illustrated was filled with women in swimsuits.

That put my fourteen-year-old mind in a hormonal frying pan. Astonished at my good fortune, I just couldn't believe they allowed stuff like this loose in the library, and I eagerly flipped through the Sports Illustrated Swimsuit Edition. In my estimation, that was not at all a bad way to spend an afternoon. Certainly better than waiting around for Jack Parker, the bus-line ass-stabbers, or going home to a house frosty with parental animosity.

So on that fateful afternoon when, unbeknownst to me, my dreams of swords and dragons, adventure and epic villains, would start, I scuttled quickly past the crowds and the junior high buildings and crossed the street to the library. Once inside, I made a beeline for the magazine section.

Of course, as it is with so many things, the anticipation is more tantalizing than the actual event. After ten minutes of ogling the tanned legs of Cindy Crawford, Christie Brinkley, and Paulina Porizkova, I got bored. I put the magazines away and wandered the book stacks, randomly pulling out books and glancing at their covers.

And then I pulled out the volume that would change my life: *The Book of Three* by Lloyd Alexander.

My wonder started with the name, I remember. I didn't understand that title, in a good way, in a way that made me want to know more. I slowly slid the book from the shelf, revealing more of the cover, and I had the oddest sense of recognition. It wasn't that I'd seen that cover before; I hadn't. But I… somehow recognized it, like I was a boy returning to the place of his birth.

In the foreground of the illustration walked a young man against a backdrop of green leaves and forest. He had a dagger in his hand, low and ready to strike.

Behind the young man, a forbidding figure dominated the picture. He sat astride a black destrier, sword in his hand. He wore a knight's plate mail on his legs, a blood red cape streamed from his neck…

And his head was a bleached skull. Living eyeballs glared down at the young boy from the rider's bony eye sockets, and antlers grew from his forehead.

I stood there, staring at the cover, and continued to feel that wispy sense of connection. I'd never seen a cover like this before, but it felt… right.

I opened it up and sat down.

Now, I had read books and even seen movies with fantasy elements before. *The Hobbit* animated movie had already been floating around for years. And I was a Disney fan of the first order, just like any California-born kid of the '70s and '80s. I was also well acquainted with Heavy Metal magazine, which wasn't at all about big hair bands like one might expect of a magazine in the early '80s with the title "Heavy Metal." No. It was, rather, a collection of R-rated sci-fi and fantasy short stories illustrated just like a DC or Marvel comic book, except with big guns, big blood, and big boobs. My brother had been an avid fan for years.

So fantasy elements were already floating around in the 1980s, but none of them had what *The Book of Three* did, at least to me. That cover was such an odd, and perfect, combination of genres for me, all blending together to create something that spoke to my soul. I mean, the skull-headed character could have been from one of the horror novels my brother often read. The plate mail armor on the figure's legs might have been from some dusty old history book about medieval knights. Even the powerful black destrier could have been from another genre, some Black Beauty equivalent.

Yet it was none of those things, and maybe all of them. It promised wonder, danger, villains, heroes. As I started to read, I discovered this story was, in fact, about a young man my age who finds adventure, magic, power, and his place in the world.

I fell in head first.

Forty minutes later, my brother found me in the stacks. He'd been waiting outside. He roughly hauled me out to The Great Pumpkin and harangued me.

But not before I checked out that book.

From that magical moment forward, everything in my life took a back seat to reading fantasy novels: school work, bullies, the increasing frequency of my parents' arguments, and even catching a rare glimpse of Tracy Goddard's legs. I constantly schemed to find a quiet place to read where no teenage pressures could touch me.

I read on the drive to school. I read before the bell rang. I snuck moments between classes. I ate lunch quickly so I could spend some of that hour in the library and turn a few more pages.

The Book of Three turned out to be the first of five novels called the *Prydain Chronicles*. I blazed through them, and I discovered more. Ravenous for whatever other stories might be found in this genre, I read *The Sword of Shannara* and the *Dragonlance Chronicles* in short order.

Junior high turned to senior high, and I continued devouring fantasy series, one of which was Piers Anthony's *Xanth Chronicles* about a fantasy world where every single person had a magical talent. Some were weak, like the ability to make a colored spot on a wall. Some were powerful, like the ability to make lightning and hurricanes.

Appropriately, Xanth was adjacent to our "real" world, which the Xanthians called Mundania (yes, Piers Anthony made me look up the word "mundane"), and every time I fell into his world, I felt more acutely just how mundane my "real" world was.

I longed to live in Xanth, get my magical talent, and become one of his heroes who always managed to save the land from the next cataclysm that always seemed to threaten it. It took a good couple of years before I combined my clearly unreasonable dreamy hope of becoming an actual fantasy hero on 1980s Earth with something I could actually do.

I could write my own story.

Maybe I couldn't be Bink or Will, the first two protagonists in the Xanth series, who fought dragons and befriended giant spiders. But writing might serve as a substitute—a pale substitute, granted—to actually being a fantasy hero. It was something at least.

It was late high school before I started coming up with my own ideas. I hatched a collaborative plan with a friend of mine who also loved science fiction and fantasy. She and I decided to write a book together. The plan was: I would write a chapter, she would write a chapter, then I would write a chapter.

The plan lasted about four chapters before she moved on to more interesting things. Like Goth music, dangly earrings, and dating.

I asked her if I could continue the story, which by then I was calling the Koric novels (after the main character). I later renamed it *The Chronicles of the Child Who Was Not,* which I thought was terribly clever at the time.

And now I think is just plain terrible.

I cannot even write that title without cringing. That vague and rambling title would become one of the first lessons I would later learn about writing: it is far better to be clear than clever.

If you can be both, good for you. But if you can't, choose clarity every time. For the sake of the reader. Please.

But thirteen chapters of the Koric Novel (see, I can't even write the title twice) got me far enough. It got me to the threshold where The Dream took hold.

This is not to be confused with The Nightmare from Chapter 1. The Dream was not a vision that came to me while I was sleeping. It captured my attention while I was wide awake. It is the lure of all good things about a potential writing career. It is the starry-eyed future nearly every author sees in their mind's eye as they embark on the writer's path.

For me, it began with what epic fantasy did for me. Those escapism stories steered me through the waters of my parents' divorce—the most impactful event in my young life by that point—in a healthy manner. In response to my family's upheaval, I could have vandalized pool rooms like my brother. I could have begun lifting weights and beating the crap out of people, like my friend Sam. I could have taken to stealing from toy stores like my friend Trent. All of them came from broken families, and all of them turned to destructive behavior. Me, I was holed up in the library reading about far off lands and heroes.

In a very real way, epic fantasy books saved my life.

By the time I finally put my own pen to paper, I was imagining doing for another what had been done for me. If I could create a land of wonder, adventure, and heroes for one young person who needed that, then it would be worth spending my life writing stories.

This was the first part of my Dream.

The second part was the lofty vision of what a successful author's life would look like. I imagined how cool it would be to have Piers Anthony's life, to live in a quirky house somewhere in Florida and write book after book. Or to have Margaret Weis and Tracy Hickman's life: millions of dollars and millions of fans waiting in anticipation for the next book.

I longed to be those people, to have their lives, to create something and put it out into the world to the excitement of readers. I longed to have the freedom that came with such wealth.

Looking back, I think a lot of my own personal emotional scars were wrapped up in the need for The Dream.

And The Dream has been, perhaps, the single greatest driver on my quest to be a writer. I've been chasing it like a mirage ever since 1988. Sometimes it has faded into the background. Sometimes it has shone in the sky like Monty Python's Holy Grail, but it's always been there.

The Nightmare gave me the courage to write. The Dream drove me to pursue a career.

3

DEMONS

LET'S TALK DEMONS.

Writerly demons come in all shapes and sizes. They are the doubts. They are the obstacles. They are the anchors that slow you down, keep you getting where you want to go as a writer. They can attack from just about any angle: your friends, your family, daily excuses, that editor who seemed mean to you, a lack of time to sit and write, a scathing review from a reader. They can show their faces in just about anyone, but every single manifestation of the demons has its roots deep within the writer themselves.

So many writers I meet want to write *Lord of the Rings, Star Wars, Game of Thrones, Dune, The Martian, Ready Player One*, or whatever their genre's equivalent is, on their first try. They want to let their inspiration, high hopes, and brilliance flow onto the page at the BANG of the starting gun. They want to prove to the world that they are the next prodigy of the written word, and of course from that moment forward, the whole world will love them. Accolades will flow. Money will rain down.

Some new writers twist themselves into knots to write this perfect book. They refuse to show their first piece to the public—or an editor, or an agent—until it's flawless. They worry over it and worry over it again until it's "ready." Sometimes for years. Sometimes forever…

Now I won't say that writing the debut, take-the-world-by-storm novel is an impossible feat. It's been done.

But I will say this: the greatest threat to a writer—especially new writers—is never finishing the book in the first place. I've met hundreds of people who intend to write a novel. Some who start. A few who even finish. But most never actually put their fingers to a keyboard.

This is a writerly demon.

Being a writer means having demons. So far as I know, there's no way to get rid of them. Every writer I know has them. They are vicious, they are constant, and they hit you where you are most vulnerable.

Because they *are* you.

The demons talk. They balk. They convince you of falsehoods. Here are some examples; see if any of these sound familiar:

"This prologue is garbage. I can't believe you'd show that to anyone."

"I'll get started on my novel after I finish college/after the wedding/after I get back from vacation/once the kids are old enough/once I retire…"

"I'm not a real writer. There are so many better writers than me. Why would anyone want to read my stuff? How can I even compete?"

I could go on and on. The demons are always around, whether you're on your 100th novel or your first.

Now let me back up again. Let's flip the calendar back to 1988. There I was, a fledgling writer with his fledgling novel in progress. It was the summer after my senior year of high school, and I lived only to write the Koric book. My fingers flew over the keyboard. The pages stacked up one after the other.

Much much later (32 years, in fact), I would write my novel *Summer of the Fetch*. In the opening scene, the main character sits in his bedroom after his high school graduation, the summer breeze wafting through the blue-and-white plaid curtains, and he sees his magical spirit fox—the fetch—for the first time.

That scene was real, plucked straight from my life. The exhilaration and fear, my burgeoning youth and the ticking clock were all part of my reality. There was only one difference between my real life and the *Summer of the Fetch* novel: instead of a fetch perched on the window sill, it was a Brother Word Processor perched on the desk, with me typing away furiously on the final scenes of the Koric book.

I have often wondered if the fetch actually *was* there at that moment. The legend has it they show up at turning points, and that was a big one for me, finishing that first book. So I have wondered. If she was, I didn't see her, and perhaps that's just the way fetches are.

I was far more focused on my book. And when I wasn't completely enthralled with that, I could only see the walls closing in on me.

My family situation had deteriorated even further.

By that summer of my senior year, my parents had not only divorced, but they'd fled to different parts of California; my father to escape a town filled with the ghosts of failure, and my mother to find a job that could actually pay the bills.

The house was in foreclosure.

In fact, as I typed those final words on my first book, somewhere a bank executive was probably drafting the paperwork to send someone to kick me out of my childhood home.

I didn't stay for the final curtain, didn't wait for them to knock on the door. I'd done what I'd needed to do.

I had typed "the end."

After those exclamatory words, I awoke from the fugue of being deep in the "otherworld" of writing. The fear of my eviction hovered ever-close, ready to pounce. In days—maybe hours—I was going to be homeless. I had no job and barely any money. My car was an old Datsun B210 hatchback with a bad drive shaft U-joint—which meant the whole thing might drop out of the car at any second—and a tendency to overheat. I should have been terrified. Except...

I wasn't. I was exhilarated. Somehow, the victory of finishing a book overshadowed the shambles of my life.

I felt the power of story in that moment. It exuded from the newly created fiction on the glowing green screen. It meant more to me—so much more—than the impending hardship descending on me. Somehow, my little stack of creation had pushed back the danger.

I was barely aware of what that meant at the time. I was a creature of instinct, but I perceived the magic of it like some barely heard voice on the wind: story could save me in a very real way.

That feeling would become part of the fabric of my life. Somehow, the joy of writing made everything else seem small.

Fresh with my magical victory, I left Durango behind. I packed up my hulking Brother Word Processor, my meager possessions, and drove out to California in my Datsun, nicknamed "The Beast." It almost overheated on every hill; I literally had to coast down the back sides in neutral to let the engine cool so it didn't blow.

Within this chaotic flurry of my life, I didn't have any bandwidth to see, much less understand, what I was learning as a novelist at that time. It was only later, when I started compiling my writing career data, that I would understand those critical, primary lessons I was learning.

Unbeknownst to me, I was absorbing the most important aspect to writing success. Lesson #1, as it were. This is going to seem so obvious you'll probably groan, but I cannot overstate its importance. The most critical part of being a successful writer is...

To write. And keep writing. To ignore the demons, whether they be doubt about your work, a lack of time, personal drama, a rejection letter from a publisher, technical difficulties, whatever.

And somehow I had that curious magic, that ability to put words on the page and to keep doing it. To not just talk about it, not just dream about it, not just tell my friends about this cool book I was going to write *someday*.

I was doing it.

Yes, my title was bad. My prose was purple. My plot was trope-y. But there was a book now where there had been nothing before.

As I left my sinking ship in Durango, I clung to my crappy little novel with the death grip of a boy who had lost everything else.

I even flew on a kind of euphoria, a feeling that everything was right in the world and nothing could get me down. I'm going to quote Neil Gaiman here, because he was right:

"Tomorrow may be hell, but today was a good writing day, and on the good writing days, nothing else matters." -Neil Gaiman

That was how I felt. I coasted on that victory for days. But soon the euphoria, as euphoria always does, went on its merry way.

The demons settled in.

They'd been gibbering and growling from the start, getting in my way, making me doubt myself. I had navigated them so far, mostly because I'd kept my manuscript to myself, but I was about to come up against the demons in the faces of other people. I was about to hand my manuscript over to an audience.

Writers, in general, are pretty sensitive people. It's part of the job description, and my thin skin was about to go through a beating.

There are many responses we writers have to criticism. See if any of these sound familiar: Acting aloof, superior. Earning degrees to prop up our internal credibility. Hopping around with a puppy-dog hope for validation (my favorite). There are probably hundreds of these knee-jerk behaviors, each designed to keep our sensitive souls from getting hurt.

A young writer's initial audience is almost always those

closest to you. This group of well-meaning people comes in three categories.

The first category is those who actually love what you do. These are the best. They tell you what they honestly love about your work, and their words will set your soul to glowing.

But unless you are that once-or-twice-in-a-generation writer who knocks the ball out of the park on your first novel, you'll meet the other two categories: the ones who didn't love what you wrote.

The first of these is the Sugar-coaters. Sugar-coaters are friends or family trying to be encouraging. I have painfully witnessed this category talking around all the things they didn't want to say, trying to offer up something positive. "Er... Yeah... This book is... y'know, pretty good. Keep at it!"

Those pitying words tell you everything you need to know. They hated it, and they're trying to spare your feelings. This kind of pandering can hurt even more than than the third and final category.

The Blunts. These friends and family are the opposite. They pride themselves on "telling it like it is" and they will not hesitate to bring a hammer down on you. My best friend in high college was one of these. His feedback on my writing was more like:

"This sucks, but you're improving."

Or...

"Look, if you're going to be such a baby about your writing, you're going to have to start diapering yourself with it."

The Sugar-coaters and the Blunts are almost equally painful, but being a writer means having to deal with both.

It was Margaret Weis, co-author of the original *Dragonlance* novels and one of my early writing mentors, who offered me a tool to deal with the Sugar-coaters and the Blunts—in fact, to deal with reviews of any kind.

"You can't listen to the bad reviews," she told me, and then after a pause. "But you can't listen to the good ones either."

I puzzled over that for years. It was a total mystery to me. How could good reviews be bad? Wasn't that people saying they liked my writing? Wasn't that positive reinforcement? Wasn't that what a writer should aspire to?

I took the "ignore the bad reviews" advice to heart. I felt it supported what I had already begun to do: ignore the haters and just write.

Later in this book—much later in my life—I finally got what she was saying about the good reviews, but at the time I was focused only on the detractors. I had discovered, and clung to, a truth that has never faded.

The key to building a body of work, to building success as a writer, is remembering that if something is not driving your work forward, be it reviews, critics, or the feedback of a friend, then it isn't useful.

I'll repeat that: if the feedback is not helping you drive your writing forward, it IS NOT USEFUL.

I had to counsel myself about this a lot because I was beset by a clamor of voices telling me how I ought to write. It wasn't so bad in high school, as most of my high school contemporaries didn't know I was writing a book and most of those who did couldn't care less.

But once I got to college, the interest and the judgements changed dramatically. In academia, the only thing more popular than students voicing their opinions about your writing was students wanting free food.

Which led into the next tool I would put in my writer's tool bag…

4

SELECTIVE IGNORANCE

LET'S TALK ABOUT SELECTIVE IGNORANCE.

Most of the time when you hear the term "ignorance," it's a bad thing, but when I say "selective ignorance," I mean it in the best possible way. This is when a person consciously chooses to ignore obstacles and focus on the Important Thing.

Selective ignorance is down and dirty. It's a riot cop's shield in a mob. It's a bayonet in the trenches. It's effective, essential, and a dismissive smack-down on the demons. It tames the distractions and helps remove interfering thoughts—and sometimes interfering people—from the process of writing. In short, it helps me get back to work.

Selective ignorance is not my original concept. It's been around for a long time, but like my inclination to just keep writing, I seemed to intrinsically understand selective ignorance.

When I got to college, the demons in my head were given external faces in the professors from whom I took writing classes. They also appeared in the faces of my friends who were aspiring writers.

As I mentioned, everyone at college had an opinion and they loved to share it. We were encouraged to voice our opinions. And great social status could be had by sounding credible, knowledgeable. So a flurry of opinions-stated-as-facts constantly floated about. Some wisdoms were generally held to be true, like the things a professor said. And if a student took a stand against a generally held wisdom, that student risked credibility within the group.

To give you an idea of what I'm talking about, one of my professors once told our creative fiction class the following:

"We won't be learning about or teaching genre fiction in this class. Genre fiction is not real fiction."

Boy, I noodled that around for quite some time.

Wasn't fiction a story about something that had been imagined? I thought that was the definition of fiction, what distinguished it from memoir, self-help or, say, a textbook.

But now I was being told that some imaginings had less value than other imaginings. To this day, I'm not exactly sure what the professor meant. It was either:

A) Real fiction is whatever academia-at-large approves as real fiction.

or

B) Real fiction is whatever the *professor* approves as real fiction.

Either way, it threw a wrench into the gears of my self-confidence. I had absolutely no interest in writing stories like *Heart of Darkness*, *A Farewell to Arms*, or *Sula*, which were examples "fantastic fiction" according to academia at the time.

I wanted to write *Dragonlance* novels. I wanted to write *Shannara* novels. And the classes offered by the college entitled "Creative Writing" or "Building Story" had slammed the coffin lid on genre fiction.

Here's a challenge: try to stand up for epic fantasy in a room of writing students who all dream of being the next F. Scott Fitzgerald or Toni Morrison.

I saw the lay of the land, and not only did I not give a rip about discussing books of that kind, I definitely didn't want to emulate them. Books like *The Grapes of Wrath* and *Moby Dick* did not save my life in junior high. Epic fantasy—high adventure and magic, warrior women and dragons, impossible quests and heroes who saved the day—had saved my life.

I could envision myself knuckling under for a time. I could see myself going along with the conventional wisdom, learning how to write like Hemingway and Conrad, but I'd be doing it only to pacify my professors long enough to get through my major and then return to what I really loved.

Or, worse than that, they might actually convert me. Then I'd spend the rest of my life chasing a dream that wasn't even my own.

So what could I do?

Well, here's what I *did* do: I stopped taking writing classes and switched my major to art studio.

I took my writing away from the cruel hammers of my professors and hearkened back to my mantra: if the feedback is not helping you drive your writing forward, it IS NOT USEFUL.

What the professors said at college rang false for me, and I'd had the courage—or stubbornness—to refute them. It was not easy, and I got a lot of eye-rolling from my peers.

"Why would you want to write like Margaret Weis when you could aspire to the magnificent brilliance that is Toni Morrison?"

But I kept writing my way, and halfway through my freshman year, I published my first short story, *Seekers*, in the *Dragonlance* anthology *Tales II, Volume 2: The Cataclysm.*

A writer's path is about as hard as it gets, but I also believe the Universe throws down bread crumbs to mark the path for us, if we keep an eye out for them. I think my refusal to submit to academic wisdom was a bread crumb. And when I finally got that *Dragonlance* short story published, it was like a handful of bread crumbs, encouraging me to keep going.

Of course, when I published, a shift happened in my peer group. None of them had a story published in a mainstream anthology that was being promoted worldwide, delighting millions of readers.

The outright condemnation of my chosen style of writing evaporated, at least to my face.

In addition, I drew admiration from those who had been quietly on my side all along but hadn't stood up to voice their opinions. Among the fantasy and sci-fi readers—of whom there were many at college—the publication of my little short story was like an elevation to royalty.

That feedback was helpful. That's what I had craved. For the career I wanted, *that* was an actual milestone.

And now I was addicted.

I never took another college writing course. Instead, I employed selective ignorance.

Instead, I wrote books.

5

THE LITTLE REBEL

IT'S TIME TO TALK ABOUT THE LITTLE REBEL.

It wasn't supposed to be time. I was going to explain the Little Rebel much later in this book, but he decided that now was the time.

He's like that.

Arguably, the Little Rebel is the part of my personality that has done the most to grow my writing career. Certainly it has saved my life, as well as my career, more times than I can count. The Little Rebel holds a unique position of power—and honor—among the plethora of voices in my head, the chorus that fuels my daily writing life.

The Little Rebel is the part of me that stands up and says "Fuck this! Fuck that! Fuck them!" when the rest of me wants to silence my voice and go along with the common wisdom.

I'd say he is the "better angel" on my shoulder, but the Little Rebel would never concede to wear white, have wings, be reasonable, or assume he was holy in any way. The Little Rebel doesn't smoke, but he would if you told him he couldn't. If you poke him, he'll not only smack your hand away, he'll put his face to your face and dare you to escalate it. The Little Rebel doesn't fear, and he doesn't care about consequences. He will use a nuclear bomb to destroy the invading army, even if the army is IN the village he's defending.

"Better to get them than give in," the Little Rebel would say.

In short, the Little Rebel is dangerous… but very useful in certain situations.

I know for a fact he's on my side, as he's saved me too many times to count, but he has no filter, no constraints, and no care for consequences. He's the voice that sabotages my weight-loss programs all the time. He doesn't like rules of any kind, and he is absolutely willing to throw the baby out with the bathwater.

He keeps me on track as a writer.

The Little Rebel was born from the Nightmare that woke me up to possibility, but honestly I think he was shaped by an encounter I had with Gary Paulson, the award-winning, New York Times bestselling author of children's and young adult stories. His most famous book *Hatchet* is about a young man whose plane crashes in the Canadian wilderness and he has to learn to survive on his own. It's a fantastic story, and you should read it if you haven't already.

When I met Gary Paulson back in 1990, the novel he was getting praise for at the time was *Dogsong*, a story about dogsledding in Alaska.

We're going to bounce back before college a little bit here (the Little Rebel doesn't care about chronological order, either).

I was a pretty good student in high school, at least by the rubric of the late 1980s, maintaining a 3.5 GPA. I wasn't rocking Valedictorian-level academics, but I hung out with the Valedictorian and Salutatorian types. I was *supposed* to go to college, at least that's what all the high school counselors and teachers told me.

But I'd spent the latter part of high school longing to get *out* of there. Of course, every high school student dreams of getting out of school. At the time, it seemed school was designed specifically to cram ideas, information, and methods of thinking into my head that *others* thought I should adopt.

After my parents' divorce, I didn't trust what others' methods were for how I should think. There was this little seedling of "knowing" that had sprouted inside me the moment I realized my parents weren't gods.

The seedling was a vulnerable little thing that whispered where I ought to go. Maybe that seedling's voice was that same voice that told me if I could hold myself together, I could fly.

Except now it wasn't just whispering in my dreams. It had broken free and could actually talk to me while I was awake, remind me what my ideal path was. I could barely hear it; I only caught its whispers from time to time, but I wanted to give it room to grow. I wanted to see not what others wanted me to be, but what this little whispering voice wanted.

That seedling of knowing was weak. It needed nurturing, and I feared that four more years of other people's thoughts and priorities crammed into my head was going to crush it. I wanted time and space to listen to it, to give it strength.

So though I got accepted to The Colorado College for early admission as my senior year wound down, I wrote back and told them I would not be enrolling.

I don't think anyone really approved. My other college-bound friends didn't understand. I mean, I'd been accepted to two of the best schools in Colorado, and I was tossing that away to…

"To do what?" one of my high school friends asked. "You're gonna travel around looking for the Fountain of Youth?"

I said, "I want to give myself some time to see what I think about this world, about life, about living. I want to empty this chaotic mind and see what the world fills it up with before I go filling it up with more stuff that *other* people think I should know."

"Uhhh… whatever, dude," was his response.

Randomly, the thing stuck in my head at that moment was

that he'd picked a bad analogy. Fountain of Youth? That had *nothing* to do with it. I wasn't youth obsessed. This wasn't about staying young. That didn't even make any sense to me. I was looking for something greater than the checklist they give you in high school, that's all. I didn't want my life to be somebody else's checklist.

What I realized later was that, no, he hadn't picked a bad analogy; he'd completely missed the point. I was telling him, "This is what's important!" And he was hearing, "Grblxxi graffxx brblixxn berf."

It simply went right over his head.

I didn't understand that exchange at the time. It would take me years to piece together why the "Fountain of Youth" comment stuck in my mind and bothered me so much. But at the time, the Little Rebel said, "Fuck 'em!"

I lit out for California. I initially stayed with my mother, my brother, and my little sister in a two-bedroom apartment in Long Beach, California. I slept next to the TV, behind my ten-speed bicycle (my most expensive and prized possession), on a few blankets on the carpet.

I didn't know how I was going to make money. I didn't know where I was going to end up; I just knew that I had to keep moving. Like a shark, I couldn't stop swimming. I felt that if I stopped, I'd drown in the greater forces all around me. As long as I was moving, scanning the terrain, eyes alert, I might stay safe.

I only stayed in California for a season. There were many adventures I won't get into now, but in less than a year, I returned to Colorado for a few months, then I was off to Portland, OR. After that, I went to Fallbrook, CA, then down to Mexico twice, and back to Colorado.

In the winter of 1990, I had seen a little of the world, working entry level jobs wherever I could find them, traveling around from town to town, state to state. I'd stocked lunchmeat and chased shopping carts at Lucky Market in California. I'd washed dishes at The Hobbit Restaurant in Portland. I'd managed a video arcade called Aladdin's Castle in

Durango.

After three years of these relatively menial tasks, my mind had finally drained of the chaos, evened itself out, and a few of my own ideas about life and what was important had risen in my mind. Not only that, but I'd written several novels.

I found that I was hungry for academia again. I reapplied to The Colorado College, got accepted again.

This time, I was going to attend.

There was time between the acceptance and actually showing up at the school, though. Many months of time. I had to find a place to cool my heels, and what better place than one of the coldest states in the Lower 48: Minnesota.

My mom was living in Bemidji at the time, so I went to live with her. Bemidji also held many wondrous and heartbreaking adventures for me, but for our purposes, we're going to focus on only one.

As was my way, I got a quick job where my mother was waitressing, and I began washing dishes at The Truckin' Cafe. About a month into my stint, I mentioned to my mom's boyfriend that I was a writer. He told me a good friend of his, Gary Paulson, was also a writer, and that he could introduce us. Gary had just come back from Alaska, and my mom's boyfriend said he'd make the introduction.

We set it up for the following week, and my girlfriend at the time, Rhian, promised to give me a ride.

I waited those seven days with keen anticipation. I'd done some research on Gary Paulson, and he was Big Time. He'd won all kinds of awards and was in every single book store I had visited.

The Dream flared to life in my mind. This could be the Big Connection that launched my career. If Gary Paulson said I was a good writer, perhaps he could introduce me to the entire world of publishing, which was an enigma to me and most of the young writers I knew.

That week went by with unbearable slowness, but the day finally came. I didn't have a car, so the plan was: I would go to work and when my shift was done, Rhian would pick me up.

She offered to drive me out there, past Black Duck (yes, there is a town called Black Duck in Minnesota) to Gary Paulson's house.

My shift ended. Rhian didn't show.

I called her and she finally picked up. This was a bad thing. Back then there were no cell phones, so if she was picking up her phone, that meant she was at home, twenty minutes away.

"Rhian, I… You were going to give me a ride. Where…? Are you coming?"

"Yeah, I can't drive out to Black Duck today," she told me.

"Rhian, I have to get out there. You said you would take me."

"Sorry," she said, not sounding sorry at all. "It's not going to work today."

Our relationship had been cooling for a few days now, and I could hear in her voice that she didn't care how important this was to me.

We talked until I realized she wasn't driving me no matter what I offered, and by then I didn't want her to. I hung up, turned away from the phone just as one of the line cooks, the scraggly, skinny one with the mullet—as opposed to the tall, pudgy one with the mullet—was headed for the back door.

"Hey Daryl, what'cha doing right now?"

"Goin' home. Why?"

I didn't particularly like Daryl. We'd never had much to talk about, and I'd often seen him staring daggers at me when Rhian showed up at the cafe—I think Daryl liked her. But I was desperate. After a five-minute negotiation wherein I promised to pay him twenty bucks, he reluctantly agreed to drive me out into the sticks to make my appointment with Gary Paulson. He wasn't sticking around, though. He was going to dump me by the side of the road and how I got back was my problem.

"That's okay," I said. I just needed to get there. What happened after didn't matter.

So he dropped me off at the end of Gary Paulson's dirt

driveway. With my thirty-five pound Brother Word Processor tucked under my arm, I marched up and knocked on the door.

Gary was a no-nonsense fellow with a round, bearded face. He wasn't forbidding per se. He smiled when he opened the door, but I really felt like I shouldn't waste his time.

We made small talk, mostly about how he knew my mom's new boyfriend and that he was happy to take a look at my work. He invited me downstairs to his den where he did his writing. Fairly quickly, he got down to business.

"Okay, show me your best piece," he said.

This, I had prepared for. I showed him my favorite chapter in my current work-in-progress: Chapter 9.

I waited for him to get sucked in, to fall into the story and continue reading. I waited for him to start nodding appreciatively, smile at the imaginative brilliance.

He read a couple paragraphs and stopped.

I felt a prickle of doom spread across my scalp.

"Okay. Show me the most recent thing you've written," he said.

Swallowing down my fear, I clumsily fumbled with the keyboard, hoping like hell I'd killed enough of the typos from this morning's chapter. I called it up and showed it to him.

Again, he read the first two paragraphs, then stopped.

My heart sank. That quickly, it was over. He'd barely read anything, and he clearly wasn't into it.

He leaned back in his chair, took off his glasses, set them on the table, and looked up at me.

I prepared for the damning criticism.

"Okay, you can write," he said.

My eyebrows raised.

"You liked it?" I asked.

"Yeah, sure. But this isn't really my genre. I'm going to forward you to a friend of mine who does this kind of stuff. Her name is Margaret."

"Okay."

"She writes books about dragons, swords. Stuff like what you've got here."

"Wait, Margaret Weis?"

"You know her?"

"I know *of* her. She's the author of the *Dragonlance* novels. Her and Tracy Hickman."

"That's the one."

My heart started thundering. "Yes, I know her! She's my favorite author!"

"Okay, well," he said with no ceremony, as though he didn't realize just how amazing it was that he knew Margaret Weis, as though it was just an ordinary thing for him. "I'm going to put you in touch."

I was beside myself.

Gary, after the business was done, became more genial. It was as though he'd gotten the tough questions out of the way—like, did I have any talent at all?—and he was relieved he didn't have to give me bad news like: Sorry kid. Go write some more and reach back out to me in a couple years. Now he didn't have to extricate himself from an awkward encounter. He could just relax.

He invited me out to his yard and showed me the converted barn where his wife painted. He told me stories about his life as a writer. He had traveled to, and lived in, a number of states including Alaska, where he'd picked up his taste for running sled dogs.

At the time, his stories seemed varied and wonderful, the life of a true adventurer. But as I have gathered more and more experience, I've come to realize that most writers have similar stories. If a writer doesn't move from place to place, all over the country or the world, then they certainly have a tendency to move from job to job, looking for their fit when, of course, their fit is being a storyteller.

For me that feeling never went away until I started writing full time, until I knew that I was throwing the best of my time, energy, and passion toward the thing that had lodged in my heart at the age of eighteen. Even now, I still have those moments of displacement, but they are few and far between.

Committing to writing is the only thing that silences it,

whether I was dedicated to write thirty minutes a morning before my 60-hour/week day job or whether it was throwing all caution to the wind and trying to make a living as a full-time author.

One of the stories Gary told me was about his time in Alaska when he went looking for fights. He said that, one night, he walked into this bar in a particularly sour mood—a bar full of rough-cut men in a similar sour mood—and announced from the doorway:

"The next asshole in this place who calls me a pussy is going to get their ass kicked!"

The immediate cacophony was:

"Pussy!"

"Pussy!"

"Pussy!"

"Pussy!"

"Pussy!"

"Pussy!"

And the brawl began.

I was a young man terrified of physical confrontation. To me, that seemed insane. Perhaps that was why the story imprinted on me more than any of his others. It was something I would never have done, and yet...

It was something I also longed to do.

I mean, I did and I didn't. After hearing that half-insane, half kinda cool story, I didn't march down to the local bar and throw myself into a redneck gladiatorial pit. But I wanted to have the courage to.

After Gary Paulson's bar story, my Little Rebel woke up. I think that part of my personality had been simmering in the back of my mind for a while, unformed. But it identified with *that* story. The Little Rebel didn't care about logical, appropriate choices—like avoiding physical mayhem and bar fights. For the Little Rebel, the "right moment" to do something was the moment it occurs to you. The "right fight" is any fight between you and anyone standing in the way of what is Important. If the catharsis Gary Paulson needed to get back to writing his stories was to brawl, then that made perfect sense to the Little Rebel.

I think the Little Rebel formed its personality in that moment, with that story. That was the moment it decided to champion my writing career without fail, to brawl with anyone who would try to stop me, time and time and time again.

And its gruff voice has always, to me, sounded a little like Gary Paulson.

6

DANCING WITH THE UNIVERSE

PART OF BEING A WRITER IS LEARNING, EXPERIENCING. It's about what I call "Dancing with the Universe," taking opportunities that are presented when they are presented and running with them. In short, it's about not knowing where you're going, but going there anyway.

After I finished college, I fell back into my wandering ways. I hadn't developed a template for what I was supposed to be as an adult, so wandering until I found that thing—whatever "that thing" was—seemed right. High school and college had filled me with a plethora of ideas of what careers I might pursue, but I didn't have a bead on what career I wanted or where I should go to start such a career. I liked exploring, though. So I decided that's what I'd do until my second-tier career presented itself.

Of course, my primary career—the career I really wanted—was The Dream. I wanted to be a bestselling, millionaire author. Deep down, though, I think I felt I didn't deserve it, that I wasn't a good enough writer to have my words take the world by storm.

Whether that was true or not, I certainly didn't know how to get from here to there. How did I orchestrate a literary windfall? How did I position an angel overhead to reach down and make The Dream come true? I had no idea.

What I discovered later was that there was no such angel. If I was going to have a shot at The Dream, it was going to take a ridiculous amount of grinding, skull-sweating, fear-soaked hard work.

At the time, though, I didn't know that. I still hoped for an angel to make my dreams reality, so I followed my "Dancing with the Universe" strategy. I went where the wind blew, which at the time meant heading out to live with my mother in Redding, CA. How unoriginal, right? The young hero, fresh out of college, heads out into the world and… runs back home.

But it didn't last long. Even though I didn't know my plans for adventure, adventure had plans for me. I soon grew restless, and an odd opportunity arose right about that time, a promise from someone I'd met in college.

In my freshman and sophomore years, a group of my closest friends and I had lived in an old Victorian house that had been converted into apartments-by-the-room.

Nothing had been updated in this dilapidated mansion. The faded blue paint was peeling. The floors creaked. Every room had different—and ugly—styles of carpet. The windows were single-paned and did little to retain heat in the winter.

And the electricity was straight from the 1940s.

A fusebox perched over an archway in the upstairs hall connecting the front of the house to the back of the house, and it contained a style of fuse I'd never seen before or since. They were like little metal hockey pucks, somewhere between the size of a quarter and half-dollar. The backside of the puck had a threaded protrusion that screwed into the sockets. The front of the fuse sported a plastic plunger that pushed in after you screwed the fuse into the fuse box. When the electrical draw overheated the fuse, the plunger popped, and the lights went out.

Unlike fuses of today, these were reusable. Of course, by

the time the plunger popped, the thing was nearly red hot. We would scurry out of our dark little warrens with a step ladder, climb up to the fusebox, quickly twist out the fuses amidst much finger blowing and cursing, and let them fall to the floor.

There were quite a few burn marks on that carpet by the time we moved out.

We would then throw the hot fuses onto a towel and carry them to the freezer, where we kept the spares. We'd swap them out and put the frozen fuses back into the fuse box.

I remember once when the fuses popped and I happened to be in the hallway. Sparks literally spurted onto the carpet.

We called this little death trap The Inferno.

The Inferno was perfect for college students who were still young enough to believe they were invincible. It was cheap, close to the college, and we knew there was no way it would burn down while *we* were inside.

Roundabout the middle of my freshman year, an older gentleman named Henk moved into Number 5. To call Number 5 an apartment was a stretch. This room was barely big enough to cram a bed and a dresser in edgewise.

To say Henk was an oddity in this barely livable fire trap was an understatement. We all watched him move in like we were watching a bespectacled condor striding up Nevada Avenue in a satin robe, smoking a pipe. We were a friendly lot, though, so we asked him what he was doing there.

Henk was an alcoholic making his way back to sobriety and holing up at The Inferno while he got back on his feet. He regaled us with many stories, not the least of which was that he used to be an airplane cargo pilot. He had run goods back and forth to some pretty exotic places during his time; he'd also been a commercial airline pilot running people back and forth from continent to continent. Also, he'd once lived in Indonesia, married a Balinese woman, and had three children with her.

His trouble with alcohol dated back to his youth, but it took its darkest turn after his wife died, and he'd left Bali to return to the States after some "bad things" he'd done during the depths of his alcoholism. He'd never explained exactly what those things were.

To the extent that we could, we included Henk in our comings and goings and sometimes our college events.

At one point, he offered me and my best friend Giles, who also lived in The Inferno, a free trip to Bali. Henk still had some kind of pull with the airline Garuda Indonesia and could get us flights. He offered us room and board, said we could live in his family's kampung—another name for a village or family complex—and eat with his family.

Giles graduated years before me and took Henk up on the offer. Years after that, and a few months in Redding with my mother, I followed suit.

If I'm going to adventure and travel, I thought, *I might as well start with the free stuff.*

This was the first of my many adventures after college. While I was in Bali, I lived in an actual kampung, slept in a little cubby room right next to a makeshift, slightly sloppy dorm-style kitchen—a microwave and a hot plate—that one of the families had taken to keeping close-by instead of taking all of their meals and keeping all their food at the large central outdoor kitchen, which was removed from the sleeping quarters.

Because of the food right outside my sleeping cubby, my room came alive with cockroaches at night. After one of them ran across my face as I slept, I staged an all-out cockroach war in the middle of the night.

I flipped on the light. The roaches scattered, but I was lightning fast in those days. My Teva rat-a-tatted like a jackhammer on everything that moved. I must have killed half a dozen cockroaches before they escaped into the dark spaces of the room—under the bed, under the dresser, under the door. Feeling like I'd sufficiently put the Fear of Todd into the little bastards, I turned out the light and went back to sleep.

As I started to drift off, I felt one of them crawl across the foot of my blanket. It hadn't even been two minutes.

In utter, creeped-out despondency, I wondered just how

many cockroaches I'd have to kill before I could get some rest. The answer?

A million. A zillion. There was no number high enough. I'd never get them all. This was a tropical climate. They would just keep coming. As long as there was darkness, they'd come creeping around. I sat on the edge of my bed, red-rimmed eyes burning with fatigue, for long minutes as I contemplated my untenable situation. How was I going to solve this unsolvable problem? I couldn't kill all the cockroaches, and they weren't going to leave me alone. What could I possibly do—?

The thought hit me all at once as I heard the little skittering movements on the floor in the dark, tentatively getting closer.

I turned the light back on. I left it on. I went back to sleep.

I was never bothered by another cockroach.

In a short time, I learned to live like the Indonesian natives. I got up with the sun. I took manual showers in the bak mandi, dumping scoopfuls of water over my head in the light blue tiled room. I ate rice, veggies, and savory meals that were sometimes made from the chicken that had been pecking in the yard the day before.

Sure, the roaches at night were creepifying, but the geckos clinging to my walls were kinda cute. My room opened to the courtyard in the center of which squatted the outdoor kitchen. The rest of the "houses," were single rooms connected to each other in the shape of a square around the kitchen. Soon, this seemed like the natural way to live. It seemed like home.

When not in the kampung, Henk and I did day trips. I roved through old temples. I saw achingly beautiful sunsets along the beaches. I climbed the holy mountain, Gunung Agung, in the pre-dawn mist. I also connected up with other travelers. One of these groups was comprised of a woman from Holland, her boyfriend from Togo, and a woman named Frederique, who hailed from Montpellier, France.

Frederique was aloof with me at first, until I made a French joke during our first dinner with Henk and the entire group. We were all sitting around the table at the completion of the meal, and I looked at her, sighed contentedly, and said, "Je suis plein."

I'd taken a crash course in French in college, and I knew enough to get around. The literal translation of my statement was "I'm full." Funny thing about French, though, and this is probably the same of any language: literal and idiomatic translations don't always match up. Literally translated into English, I'd said I was done eating.

To an actual French person who knew the idioms, I'd just said, "I'm pregnant!"

Frederique raised a long-suffering eyebrow and opened her mouth to correct the dumb American. But I'd been watching for that. Before she could speak, I winked at her and finished with, "comme an oeuf," which throws the phrase back into the idiomatic, indicating I was stuffed with food, and not a fetus.

She closed her mouth, and for the first time her eyes glimmered with interest. She cocked her head and smiled at my joke.

"There is more to you than meets the eye, I think," she said.

From that moment on, Frederique and I hit it off, and after the group broke up because of different schedules, she and I traveled together for most of my time in the country. At the end of nearly two months, I headed back to the U.S., but I couldn't stop thinking about her. So after lingering for only a few weeks back in Colorado Springs and, at an invitation from her, I flew out to Europe to be with her.

While I was there, I visited Paris, Montpellier, and Marseille. We went on an adventure with Frederique's friends to a beautiful house in the Pre-Alps. Those lush forests took my breath away. I practically had an out-of-body experience while I lagged behind the group during a hike. They wended down the path and then up a slope on the other side as I lingered, watching them, and I realized I'd never seen anything in real life that looked more like a scene from Lord of the Rings. A line of adventurers hiking up a hill against a backdrop of misty green trees. If they'd had swords and cloaks, it could have been the Fellowship of the Ring, I swear.

Frederique and I also visited the friends we'd met in Indonesia with a jaunt up to the Netherlands. We visited the famous Red Light district, browsed a few museums where I gravitated to the Rembrandts (I loved Rembrandt), drank wine, and soaked in the camaraderie of our very own multi-national fellowship.

"We are international!" Frederique would exclaim.

While in Europe, I sharpened my French speaking and had a fantastic time noting all the differences between French and American culture. For one, I was shocked to discover that in Frederique's high school experience, there were no cliques.

I mean, the movie *The Breakfast Club* defined my high school years, illustrating with startling accuracy the clear-cut dividing lines between teenage social groups. For my part, I had always belonged to Brian's Egghead clique. I was not cool, not popular, not into sports, I didn't party, I always did my homework, and I played Dungeons and Dragons on the weekends with the other nerds. So whenever I watch that movie, I always identify with Anthony Michael Hall's Brian character. When I explained this to Frederique and asked her what clique she'd been in during high school, she seemed mystified by the whole concept.

"You didn't have any groups that hated other groups at your school?" I asked. "Like jocks and nerds, cheerleaders and goth girls?"

She just shrugged and said, "It was mostly just girls versus the boys."

That stuck in my head. What had seemed such an immutable part of growing up was in fact just an American cultural twist. It made me wonder just how many other things I took for granted as an American that might be completely absent in another country. And how many things existed in other cultures that were completely absent in America?

That opened my eyes. These adventures, more than anything else, helped me frame the characters in my writing. Every time I crafted a character that was a carbon copy of other characters I'd read, or other characters I had created myself, I stopped and forced myself to think outside of my own frame of reference, to allow for things I didn't know or didn't understand.

To this day, even when I have conviction about something, I always leave back a 10% chance that I am wrong, that I might be unaware of something. I mean, when I'm talking about a subject, or when I'm engaging with a group of people, I can project confidence. I can be "absolutely certain" with the best of them. But in the back of my mind, I always wonder what might change my mind, if there's some piece I may not have seen yet. Europe and Indonesia taught me that.

Frederique taught me that.

7

TRUSTING THE VOICE

I'VE TALKED ABOUT A LOT OF VOICES UP TO THIS POINT. The voice telling me to hold myself together so I could fly. The spiritual seedling whispering of another life as yet undefined by parents or high school teachers. The Little Rebel. Each of these voices, initially untested, eventually became essential to my journey.

There is one voice I haven't mentioned yet, though, a voice that wrenches my gaze away from what I think I "ought" write—what I think would be acceptable—and bids me write what is true.

Stephen King talks about this in his book *On Writing*. He mentions writers should write about whatever the hell they want to write about, as long as it's honest.

In my post-college wandering and experimentation, I didn't yet believe in that voice, but I was about to have a near-death experience that would turn me from skeptic into true believer.

After a month in France, Frederique and I parted company. I wasn't going to live in France forever, and she wasn't coming to the States. That was the fall of 1995. I returned and moved to Flagstaff, AZ with Giles. He had contracted to do work with a company called MFP, the same company that he and I had worked for in college.

Two years prior, during the summer between my sophomore and junior years in college, Giles inspired me to run away to Oregon. That's when we discovered this company for the first time. With MFP, we got jobs climbing inside supertankers while they were at port, after they had been drained of their cargo. For $18/hour, a nice bit of pay back then, we would go inside the tanks and hang cables so that hull-inspecting teams could run Spider motor platforms—like the ones used to wash windows on skyscrapers—up and down the hulls to make sure the steel had no cracks.

There was a reason the per-hour pay was so high. MFP was a fly-by-night operation. The vetting process for qualified personnel was non-existent. The safety precautions were laughable. The job was flat-out dangerous.

The fall-block equipment to protect the climbers was, essentially, a cable attached to a tripod with a spring-catch system. The tripod was set up over a butterworth—a hole about the size of a human head that gave limited access through the deck—and the cable was fed through into the yawning, enormous oil bays below.

The climber—me—would then attach the fall-block cable to the back of his harness. If I were to slip off the wall, the weight of my body was supposed to trigger the spring-catch system and it would lock up. I'd then dangle over the killing drop until, I suppose, someone came to get me or I swung over and grabbed onto the wall.

Also, these fall blocks were rated for 225lbs. Yeah. That's a bit alarming to a guy who weighed nearly 200lbs. I wasn't at all sure if that cable would hold if I took a decent sized whipper with some slack in the line.

These fall blocks, while pretty smooth during the first twenty feet of cable, had a spring that was designed to pull the cable back and coil it on the reel once the climber had unclipped. That meant the longer the cable, the higher the tension on the line as the spring wound tighter and tighter. When I'd climbed twenty feet distant from the fall block's butterworth, the tension was tight but manageable. At fifty feet, it felt like someone was hauling at the back of my harness. At seventy feet—about the max distance—it was a constant fight. I had to pull myself onto the wall almost as hard as I had to pull up against gravity.

Ridiculous. Exhausting.

As a result, many of the climbers would just unclip from the fall block at about thirty feet and say, "Fuck it." They would rather trust their own arms and judgment than fight the fall block.

Also, after climbing through a few lightning holes—man-sized holes through the steel sheets of support that kept the shape of the ship—it effectively rendered the fall blocks useless. I mean, if you climbed far enough away from the fall block, you'd hit the ribbed steel floor of the tank before the line pulled tight.

My first day on the job in Astoria, a newbie fell and broke his leg. He'd been wearing his fall block cable.

They called an ambulance to haul him away, and I never saw that guy again. To my knowledge, he showed up excited for this new job, busted his leg, and that was the rest of his summer right there. Nice day for him. Also, I'm relatively certain he never received a penny from MFP, either for his twenty minutes of work or the medical bills.

Now let me illuminate the conditions inside the tanker. Most of the jobs were in Portland, and Portland in the summer is about ninety degrees with a hundred percent humidity on the top of the ship's deck. Inside the steel ship… that's a whole different environment. Without its cargo, the ship is essentially a big steel box. You stick a big steel box under the sweltering sun all day, and you've got yourself an oven.

Down in the tanks, the heat was thick and debilitating. Completely enclosed with no cooling breeze, the tanks were a hundred and ten degrees, easily. Depending on whether I was in a ballast tank or an oil tank, it either smelled like brine and twenty-day-old fish or the nefarious chemical fumes of the benzine they used to clean out (most of) the oil.

I've been describing the immediate physical dangers of this job, but let's not forget about the benzine fumes. At the time, I didn't know what a long-chain mono-carbon was. I would later discover that prolonged exposure to benzine fumes was an invitation to a cancer-riddled future.

But let's skip right past that and move on to the moment in question, a frighteningly magical moment.

So there I was at the end of a long, exhausting day, at the top of the last bay in the last tank. I'd spent all my strength getting to this point, having hung cables in the dozen other bays in this tank already. My muscles twitched from the torture I'd put them through after eight hours of climbing up the equivalent of a hundred-foot building, then rappelling down, then climbing up another hundred-foot building, then rappelling down. Over and over and over.

The hottest part of the tank was the top, right up against the deck where the sun was broiling the other side. The air above the deck might have been in the nineties, but under that two-inch thick steel, it was a hundred-and-twenty degrees, and the ratholes where I placed the hooks were right up against it. I sometimes had to get so close to the killing heat that my eyes involuntarily closed.

My body was slick with sweat, my tank top and shorts were so wet I could have just emerged from a swimming pool. I was undoubtedly suffering from mild heat stroke by then, and I simply wasn't thinking clearly. It's important to note that I—unlike most of these testosterone-fueled, chest-beating, dock-worker climbers—wore my fall block every time I climbed.

But this was the end of the day, the last bay of the last tank, and I was the furthest from the tripod. My "spotter"—the poorly paid, unskilled dock worker whose job it was to play out the slack in the fall block, grip the cable with gloved hands, and try to keep some of the tension off my back—had been falling asleep at the job. I was literally being pulled off the wall, and I was sick of it.

Safety first, though, right?

I'd just hung the last safety rope—the rope that the inspectors on the spider motors would put through their fall-block equipment—from the rat hole in the under deck. I pulled its length out, funneled it through my Figure 8 and clipped that to my D ring. I set my weight on it gently and bounced a few times to make sure it was secure.

Then I clipped free of that damned fall block.

I drew a breath of relief as the cable attachment whipped away from me, clanging through the lightning hole and vanishing into the black. The spotter hadn't been holding the line at all. Fucker.

I started rappelling down.

As I mentioned, I was a hundred feet up, and it was brutally hot right up against the underside of the deck. The temperature dropped ten degrees after the first ten feet I descended and ten degrees after the second ten feet. I looked up at the retreating hot plate of the under deck, and I felt relief. I was done for the day. The bottom of the tanks were damned near air conditioned by contrast, as they were submerged deep in the cool water. I longed to get down there, and soon after out of these benzine fumes.

Hell, I longed to be away from this whole damned job. What was I even doing here? Four weeks ago, I'd been in a dance class at The Colorado College with a dozen beautiful women. What was I doing among the cussin', spittin', fartin' dock set whose idea of a good time was getting drunk, fighting, and seeing who could lose the most teeth—

I felt a tingle at the back of my head, like a light finger brushing.

I assumed it was sweat. I didn't even give it a thought.

Anyone who has climbed before will know that I was in the process of committing several mistakes.

First, I'd let go of my fall block protection at the last moment. I was attached to the new safety rope, after all.

Second, I was rappelling, and I was looking upward, my

mind wandering. When rappelling, you should look down so you can not only see where you're going, but you can see the play of the rope. Or even better, I should have alternated glances up to check that things were good, and then down to see where I was headed.

Third, I was moving really fast. I was thinking about *after* I was done in the tank. I was thinking about *after* my job was done. All I wanted was to get out of the heat. I was not paying attention to the job that, actually, wasn't finished yet.

That feathery touch came again, and this time I noticed. That wasn't sweat. That was…

What was that?

A little voice in my head said, *"Check your equipment."*

I answered the voice, because when you're heat-addled, you answer the voices in your head.

"I built it right," I replied inside my own mind, referring to the rope I'd looped around the Figure 8. I'd done it right. It was secure.

"Check your equipment," the voice whispered again.

"I don't need to check my equipment. Everything's fine. I did it right."

"Check your equipment," the voice whispered again. It was gentle, insistent, and even a little bit sad. Like the voice of a loved one standing over your grave.

Now during this conversation, I had descended a good fifty feet. The temperature of the air had dropped from a hundred and ten to a relatively reasonable eighty degrees—which felt like fifty degrees to my poor abused brain—and I suddenly began thinking straight again.

A different voice entered the conversation, the voice of reason.

"Hey Todd, could it hurt to stop for a second and check your equipment? If you're right and you built that loop correctly, you'll lose maybe fifteen seconds. What's fifteen seconds? If you're wrong… Well, you might just save your own life."

My quickly cooling brain had no witty rejoinder for that. That was just straight up horse-sense.

Forty feet up from the steel bottom, I braked, pulling the slack in the safety rope down against my thigh, binding up the Figure 8 as it was designed. I swung into the wall and braced my feet against one of the shelves. I looked at my equipment. The loop was right. I'd built it correctly; it was a perfectly safe rappelling mechanism… My gaze went past the setup to my gloved brake hand, which gripped the remaining rope.

The final foot of the rope.

Its dirty, orange-taped ends stuck out of my fist like pigtails. I swallowed hard.

I was still forty feet above the ugly steel floor of the tanker, which was punctuated every six feet by three-foot-tall girders that could break a man's back like a toothpick, especially a man falling from a height of forty feet.

I leaned into the wall and sucked into it like hot shrink wrap.

For a moment, I didn't understand what was going on. It made no sense. The rope was too short! The safety rope was too short!

Then I realized what had happened.

A ship curves. A little at the stern, but notably at the bow. And an oil tanker makes the absolute most of its space, so the tanks go all the way to the front. Unlike the tanks in the middle of the ship, the ones toward the bow are shorter, the foremost only fifty feet tall.

This rope had been designed to be put, and was supposed to have been put, in the forward tanks. This damned company had hired somebody who didn't know the difference—or didn't care. Or maybe to someone who wasn't thinking too much about it, a sixty-foot rope probably looked a lot like a hundred-foot rope when coiled on the deck.

I left the short rope dangling in the air, useless and deadly, and I climbed carefully down those forty feet to the bottom, thinking about how I'd almost died. If I'd kept going for a half second more—just a half second!—the short rope would have slithered through my fist, through the Figure 8, and I'd have gone backward into a free fall all the way to the bottom, where

I'd have hit head first. It would have killed me. And if by some miracle I'd survived, I'd have been broken forever.

I couldn't stop thinking about it. For days afterwards, for weeks, I kept thinking about that little scratch at the back of my head. I kept thinking about that voice.

Don't believe in angels? In fetches? In the Universe looking out for you? Well, I can tell you for certain there's something out there.

That swelteringly hot, bone-chilling day in Portland made me a believer. If there was no supernatural power looking out for me, then my subconscious was working at supernatural levels.

That voice, whatever it was, saved my life. It also taught me an incredible lesson about writing: listen. Navigating the story coming up from my imagination, from my soul, requires listening. Even the smallest voice can matter. And sometimes it matters the most.

And sometimes it doesn't seem to be about what it's actually about. Sometimes warnings about checking your equipment are just words to get you to LOOK DOWN.

There have been so many times in my writing career where I've asked myself:

"Where is this story going?" And I won't realize why until the end of the chapter, and in some cases the entire book.

Without that voice, I would have fallen that day. That's the truth. And I would most likely have died. But I listened. And I didn't. It is a lesson I never forgot.

So two years later when I returned to Flagstaff after France, I still couldn't stop thinking about that incident, about that angel scratching softly at the back of my neck, and I spent the winter writing a book about her.

8

WRITING FROM THE HEART

A GREAT MANY OF MY WRITING CHOICES AROSE from that little voice that saved my life in Portland, probably more than I can recall, certainly more than I ever realized. In fact, that voice might be running in the background all the time like a computer operating system. I only *see* about 10% of what it's doing. An enchanted subconscious, if you will. A well-trained intuition that pointed out the path.

But there were some decisions I had to make on my own.

Ever since I formulated my version of The Dream, I'd longed for that writer's paradise. The money, the mansion, the accolades, seeing my book titles sitting all over the tops of bestseller lists, book signings in every book store in cities big and small, a European tour…

I wanted all of that. I still do, and I sometimes imagine that no matter how much success I have, I will always want an updated version of The Dream, a greener pasture that's just out of reach.

But as I've looked back on my path, the weird twists and turns it's taken—so much of it seeming random chance—I've realized I made decisions from the heart almost every time. It's true that sometimes I made choices out of greed, fear, or expediency, but mostly I made them from the heart.

No matter where it came from, every choice taught lessons. My ignorance has been battered into wisdom again and again. I've wasted more than a few days, months, years trying to use my big brain to create the clever shortcut to Shangri-La, when the only real way to advance was to follow my heart.

I could have made a lot more money at several crossroads in my life by not following my heart. I could have nabbed this writing contract here, or that writing opportunity there by giving up something that would have hurt my heart, maybe permanently. But what I came to find is that when I made decisions from the heart, whether the outcome is loads of cash or raiding the change-jar to scrape up enough pennies for an evening of Chinese food for me and my sweetie, I loved the result. Those results were easy to stand by.

The rubric that has popularly come to define American Success—if you're rich and decadent, you win—had little hold on me early on in my life, probably because of my mother, who was magic. She could make a fear-prickling, poverty-stricken flight from Colorado to California an adventure. She showed me that excitement, happiness, and satisfaction rose from within. So I kept one eye on the scenery, absorbing the beauty whether I was looking at a gray and oily industrial park in Denver or a breathtaking twelve-thousand-foot mountain vista at the top of Copper Mountain.

I also found the more I answered the voice of my heart, the louder it became and the more my internal satisfaction grew, no matter the challenge. I wasn't dependent on pop culture, the government, or corporate advertising to define happiness for me or deliver it to me. I carried it with me.

One of my biggest lessons was setting boundaries for my writing career, following my heart instead of jumping at the shiny opportunity. This lesson came during my time in Flagstaff.

I was given an opportunity to co-write a novel with one of

my favorite authors from my teenage years. The co-writing devolved into a ghostwriting credit (that is to say no credit), and I learned something new about myself.

After writing an entire novel, practically by myself, and then receiving no credit, I felt a sour taste in my mouth that followed a decision made from the desire to hop a few rungs on my way to The Dream.

I didn't like that taste at all.

Now don't get me wrong. Ghost writing is a perfectly viable and often lucrative path in the writing world. Not for a second do I mean to imply that one should not ghost write. For some, it is the perfect opportunity.

But I found that it was unequivocally not for me.

I did my job, got paid my money, and saw that novel flow down the river with someone else's name on it.

I swore I'd never do that again.

That lesson has come back to me time and again. I wasn't offered more ghost writing opportunities, but if I had been, I would have said no. It helped me cement my creed: if it doesn't serve my writing career—the writing career I envision—I'm not spending time on it.

This is a tricky position to take. Sometimes situations are perfect for my path, but they don't look like it. Sometimes they are poison, but they look perfect. In those instances, it's important to be able to hear what your heart wants, and to have the courage to follow it.

I've gone down enough poison paths, turned around at enough dead-ends, lost and confused that I have no interest in doing it again. I try to keep my intention focused on the long term goal. The Dream that is *my* dream, not something that only *seems* like it can take me there faster. I think Neal A. Maxwell said it best:

"Never give up what you want most for what you want today."

When you're young and hungry, it's easy to sell your magic for pennies. It's easy to trade everything when you glimpse The Dream. But don't sell your magic short.

Listen to your heart. Always.

9

THE HUNT FOR MAGIC

ONE OF THE GREATEST ADVENTURES I EVER HAD hijacked my best intentions to write.

I'd graduated college, and I spent a frustrating winter in Flagstaff stocking shelves on the graveyard shift at Walmart. I later worked at a Sign-a-Rama, had love affairs with a willful norse pagan and a stained-glass-artist/snowboarder, and learned how to ride a motorcycle.

I was so poor that I lived in a shack where one of the walls was literally an uninsulated piece of plywood. I later lived in a five-bedroom house in the suburbs with five other friends. We had squirt-gun wars that ranged all over the neighborhood.

When that group split up and went their separate ways, I moved back to Redding, CA to be close to my mom. I worked at a hair care company called KMS, published again in another *Dragonlance* anthology as well as a fractured fairy tale anthology called *Twice Upon a Time*.

I got promoted at KMS, and then got promoted again. I earned a very respectable salary for doing something I'd never envisioned doing; I was a Brand Coordinator in the marketing department. I don't think my colleagues truly understood me. I would often crack jokes that went without a laugh, and some of the things I took ironically, they took quite seriously. But I was a hard worker and smart enough to pick up whatever they threw at me, so I kept getting promoted.

But eventually, I got itchy feet again. I had felt for some time that this wasn't my place, and I wanted to get out of there. Excelling in an area that wasn't my calling was always exciting at first—I have always loved the positive feedback of accolades—but eventually it paled, and soon it became like little bamboo shoots slowly pushing under my fingernails as my heart began to speak again.

If I was going to be a novelist, what was I doing as a Brand Coordinator?

At the end of the summer, I quit my job, moved out of my apartment, and set out on the road again.

I packed everything I had into a few duffles and flew out to Hawaii to try to re-ignite an old flame from college. The flame did not re-ignite, and I returned from the islands with a heavy heart. I spent New Years Eve in Colorado, ringing in the New Year of 1999 with all of my friends from the Flagstaff House. Afterward, I embarked on a frozen winter road trip through Minnesota and North Dakota. Both are beautiful states, but I do not recommend a road trip through them in January.

Despite all of this adventuring, my grandest adventure was nearing, and I wasn't yet aware of it.

I returned to Placerville, CA where I planned to get a job with as little responsibility as possible. I was thinking dishwashing; it's hard to get promoted out of dishwashing. I planned to free up my thinking to write. It was time to get serious. I needed to stop messing around with these better-paying jobs that took my brainpower and expected my loyalty. I was going to force myself to be an underachiever so I could give the best of myself to my real career.

I rode my motorcycle, a black Yamaha SR-500, into town. The thing was a great get-around-town bike, a 500cc one-cylinder engine, which made it *sound* like twice the bike it actually was.

I got set up with a couple of roommates, but before the job hunt, I took a quick detour to visit a friend from college, Shona, who had invited me to come see her in San Francisco. This would be my last hurrah before settling in and getting to work.

I never made it back to Placerville.

While I was in San Francisco Giles, who had been screenwriting in L.A., showed up on Shona's doorstep after I'd been there for only a few days. Turns out he'd had a revelation in Los Angeles, had hopped in his battered old truck, and driven up to Placerville to find me. My roommates told him where I'd gone, and he lit out for San Francisco next.

I was relaxing in Shona's little kitchen/living room in her little apartment when he rang her doorbell.

"Uh, Todd, it's for you," she said when she answered the door.

I was stunned. "For me? Nobody knows I'm here."

I reached the door and saw Giles standing there.

"Wanna come to New York City?" he asked.

"What?"

"Wanna come to New York City?" he repeated.

I opened my mouth but didn't answer. I mean, I was done adventuring. Between my heartbreak in Hawaii, the New Year's Eve party in Colorado, the road trip through the frozen north, and the motorcycle ride out to San Francisco, I had seen enough adventure for a while. I just wanted to settle down and get back to writing.

"I'm not going to New York City," I said. "I'm going to wash dishes and write books."

"Wrong answer," he said. "Let me tell you why."

Shona's eyebrows were permanently raised; she had a "What the hell is going on here?" expression, but this was my best friend. Clearly something had sparked inside him to cause him to jump in his truck and drive all the way up here.

We brought him inside and he told me about his

revelation. His screenplay writing career was going nowhere in L.A., and he'd had a vision while tripping on mushrooms in a park where he'd almost lost the necklace I'd given him, which I'd procured in Bali after climbing the holy mountain.

He held it up, and it glittered in the afternoon light that slanted through the window. After searching through a field of dried leaves where he'd lost it, he'd finally found the necklace, and a message had come along with it.

"We may never get another chance to look for magic together. Our lives are about to be set in stone. We've graduated. We've floated around doing whatever these past few years. But we've never taken that chance and simply put everything on hold to find magic. Real magic in the world. Let's go. Let's go from coast to coast in a search for it, and if we don't find it by the time we reach the Atlantic, so be it. Then you're free to go."

"I'm in," I said.

I'm pretty sure Shona thought we were batshit crazy, but I admired Giles's brass by tracking me down and spilling his inspiration. I mean, not only did he tell me his wild story, but he'd told it in front of Shona and her friend, who also happened to be over at the time.

We headed out that same day.

We started at The Getty Museum in L.A., looking at fine works of art, then we got into Giles' battered old Ford truck, which we'd named The Drudge Skeleton after a card from *Magic: The Gathering*. In the game, a Drudge Skeleton is a lowly, Strength 1 creature that could be resurrected again and again using dark magic.

Giles equated money to this dark magic, which actually fit perfectly. Every time the car broke down, he threw money at it, and it started running again.

Now, the idea of getting serious about my writing had been percolating for quite some time. I mean, down and serious. I'd wanted to be a writer since high school. I'd run with the writing crowd in college. I'd added to my growing body of work at all other times.

But I'd never planted my flag in the ground and said, "This is my career choice! I shall defend it against all comers!" I'd been too timid to do that, too afraid it wouldn't work out. There were more than a few things standing in my way, including believing I wasn't good enough to publish.

I know I know. I'd already been published, and in well-known anthologies. I'd ghostwritten a novel for one of my childhood heroes.

But Impostor Syndrome knows no logic. It has dogged my steps through every phase of my career. It didn't matter if I published a short story or twenty-seven novels. It didn't matter if I hit the Amazon #1 bestseller list or won the Colorado Authors League Award for Writing Excellence. There would always be this little voice in the back of my head telling me I'm not a real writer yet. There would always be another bar to reach that "real authors" were reaching. There would always be another goal post that kept moving further away.

But as Giles and I went east, stopping in Denver, Minneapolis, Boston, and finally in New York City, not only hadn't we found the magic we sought, but my urge to truly test myself in the publishing world was growing.

As we reached New York City, home of the big publishers, I realized I wanted to start that next phase. I didn't want to give my writing just to family and friends. It was time to see what a publishing industry professional was going to think of my work. I was ready to try marrying up my literary talents with money.

As I settled into the everything-everywhere-all-at-once culture of New York City, where there was more breathtaking art, aspiring artists, off-the-chain parties, fascinating friends, and passionate lovers than I'd ever thought possible, I began to think about those publishers, about doing more than just taking a handout from Gary Paulson, about daring to throw myself onto the slush pile and see if I could rise to the top.

I made several mistakes right up front.

First, I became completely distracted by New York City. Don't shame me. It could happen to you. I was footloose and eager to experience. College had been a high point in my life, and New York City was college on speed, on steroids, on the gods' own ambrosia.

I soaked up the culture, worked with the artists, attended the parties, hung with the friends, and fell into my fair share of arms. I continued writing, but adjusting to the big city took a lot of energy and time, and I'd been in NYC for most of a year before I got back to writing.

Once I did, I thought about doing more than just building my craft. It was time—and what better place?—to start trying to find an agent.

This was when I made a classic newbie mistake.

I had looked through the Writer's Market and I'd asked Margaret Weis who she thought were the best agents in the biz. She said that, for fantasy, The Donald Maass Literary Agency was the cream of the crop.

I looked at my collection of novels, selected *Wildmane*, and selected what I thought was my most compelling chapter, then sent it to the Donald Maass Literary Agency.

It was Chapter 9.

"sigh"

So… If you get no other bit of wisdom from this chapter, let it be this: don't send Chapter 9 to a potential agent. Don't send Chapter 9 to *anyone*. It painted me as an amateur instantly.

Here's the truth: If your book's Chapter 1 isn't good enough to parade in front of an agent or editor—to parade in front of the *world*—then your Chapter 1 isn't good enough to be in your book. Rewrite it until it IS that good, then send it.

I got a stock rejection from the Donald Maass Literary Agency, and I deserved it.

I dove back under the bed. The mistaken lesson I took away from this was that my writing was crap and I didn't deserve to be published.

The lesson I *should* have taken from this was to retool, rework, and resubmit (this time hopefully with Chapter 1).

I'd built some confidence in my craft, but my confidence in properly showcasing my own work to the professional set was at about 0 out of 10.

What the whole scenario should have done was push me to work harder, but despite all my talk and even all my work, I hadn't fully committed to becoming a writer yet. I was still hoping to "get noticed" while I worked whatever jobs came my way and enjoyed the flush of my youth.

I simply wasn't there yet.

But it was coming.

10

NEW YORK

I NEVER PLANNED TO HAVE KIDS.

I mention this because I hit a turning point in New York City that drove me back to Colorado, which was where I finally started taking my writing seriously. For me, the evolution of moving from amateur to professional writer was wrapped up in having a family.

I didn't have what it took to be a successful writer, not yet. And it wasn't because I lacked the things that my Impostor Syndrome told me I lacked, like talent, skill, or a work ethic.

What I lacked was an unflinching commitment. I hadn't planted that flag into the hill, announced to myself and the world that I wasn't messing around anymore, that I was going to be a writer or I was going to die. I kept inventing fallbacks for my as-yet-unrealized writing career.

Since high school, I had been roving around and taking my opportunities and pleasures in the shape and frequency the Universe doled them out. It was a glorious time. I had no expectations, and when you have no expectations, it's hard to be disappointed.

I made the most of my opportunities as I chased happiness.

What started my journey toward being a family man was a moment I experienced in a New York City supermarket parking lot.

I mentioned before that New York was full of wonderful distractions. Not only were there as many flavors of entertainment—theaters, museums, architecture, concerts, cafes, bars, parties—as a person could imagine, but there were so many amazing women and so many fun trysts to be had. These trysts suited my vagabond lifestyle well, and I didn't see myself ever settling down. I loved the cycle of meeting someone new, getting to know them, spending intimate time with them, letting the relationship come to its zenith, then moving on to the next relationship.

But the truth was, I wanted my soulmate. I simply wasn't willing to settle for someone who wasn't her, and I also had no interest in being a monk in the meantime. I was perfectly willing to have fun with whomever wanted to have fun with me, no strings attached.

I always told my prospective lovers this right up front.

I had more takers than I had any right to expect. I loved each of them in my no-strings fashion, and I enjoyed each of them thoroughly. I'd like to believe that each of them enjoyed me as well.

I had no intention of changing this unless I hit the jackpot and met that one perfect life partner. I wasn't about to partner up with someone and have children if I wasn't sure because I was terrified of picking the wrong person and going through a divorce… especially with kids.

I wasn't going to do to a child what had been done to me.

So while I was in New York, I was the good-time guy, free for the taking but not for the having. I wasn't interested in kids, wasn't interested in settling down. And I was more than happy with that. My adventures filled me up, set my inspiration alight.

But one fateful evening as I was walking up to the supermarket to get my weekly staples—I was actually daydreaming about a liaison I'd had the previous night—I saw a guy about my age walking out of the supermarket. To this day, I don't know why he caught my eye. Maybe he reminded me of me: a sure stride, a relatively unconcerned look.

Suddenly, a little girl of about six or seven ran up behind him. She reached up and took the man's hand. He accepted her hand like it was the most natural thing in the world, looked down with a smile so warm and genuine that I stopped walking.

He slowed his stride to match hers, and she swung their hands between them. It was obvious the little girl adored him, and he adored her. I hadn't looked at such a thing like that before; I hadn't ever cared. This time, a little voice in my head said, *"Awwww…"*

I thought, *"That looks so… nice."*

Then I came to my senses.

What was I thinking? That was *family*. That was *children*! That was responsibility and commitment and being tied down. That was choosing the same thing, day after day, for the rest of my life.

That's not who I was. That wasn't what I did.

But that moment, that scene, cracked my armor. The notion of settling down began to spread through my mind.

Six months later, I left New York.

11

THE AGENT

I WANTED TO SETTLE DOWN. The little girl holding her daddy's hand was a catalyst, and I returned to Colorado with the feeling that I wanted to put down roots. I didn't have a plan. I didn't know what "settling down" looked like, but I knew I wanted it to happen there. And I wanted it to happen now.

That one moment in that supermarket parking lot set off a chain of events for me, and everything fell together like it was destined. I did, indeed, find my perfect life partner. How I met her, and how we came to be together, is another story altogether. But for the purposes of this narrative, I moved back to my beloved Colorado, got engaged, bought a house, got married, and had a baby.

This became my crucible. It was what I'd been avoiding for years. I'd wanted to experience life, unconstrained by obligation. I'd wanted to allow space to write without any other responsibilities in my way. My day job track record reflected this. I'd never spent more than two years at any job.

But over the next twelve years in Englewood, I worked at

only two day jobs: the Juvenile Diabetes Research Foundation and the American Diabetes Association. I focused on stability for my children, for my wife, and ensuring that love—and decisions from the heart—were the staples of my family unit.

I was still writing, taking time here and there to put words on paper. Giles had moved back to Colorado ahead of me, and after I finished *Threadweavers* he and I got to kicking around the idea of a collaborative project.

Giles and I had already collaborated on a number of works in college and after, and we fell back to the brainstorming with zeal. It was like playing D&D with my best friend, always a blast.

Also, I'd finally overcome my fear of the business side of publishing after my Chapter 9 Query Letter Debacle. Now that I was settled in one place, I decided to take a run at that hill again.

In 2002, a friend of mine turned me on to the Pikes Peak Writers Conference (PPWC), and I decided to go. It was mind-blowing. I was like a kid who'd only seen one or two toys in my life and now I'd suddenly entered the toy store. Back then, the publishing industry had been a complete enigma to me but now, suddenly there were no walls between me and the people on the *inside*.

Agents were mythical in my head. I'd seen them as heroes that, if they took a liking to you, would guide you through the misty jungles of publishing. And editors from the Big Seven (the big NYC publishing houses at that time) were like unicorns.

But this conference had them all. Professional agents. Editors from Random House, Macmillan, Penguin, HarperCollins, Simon & Schuster, Tor, and their imprints.

I'd prepared badly for the conference, having no idea what to expect. I didn't have a plan for what I wanted to learn. I hadn't set up any pitch sessions ahead of time. But I rolled with my new situation and made the most of it. I talked to agents and editors at the hotel bar. I was pretty sure I was breaking the rules by doing that, but by the time I left that year,

I had three requests for submission.

I sent them all *Wildmane.*

They all rejected it.

In 2003, I returned to the conference, and this time I was prepared. I took pitch sessions *and* I jawed at the bar. I pulled people aside in the hallways while they were on the way to their workshops and panels. I got nine requests for submission.

I sent them all *Wildmane.*

They all rejected it.

By 2004, I'd finished the *Threadweavers* series, Giles and I had begun working on our new project, *Heir of Autumn,* and we had twelve sparkling new chapters out of a planned sixty that we both thought were pretty good. We decided we were going to both set up pitch sessions, divide our labor, and hit twice as many potentials at PPWC than I had in the previous year.

One of the first things we did at the conference was join a Read and Critique session. This was where a trio of industry professionals—agents, editors, publishers, or published authors—would sit at the front of a room of about thirty aspiring authors. One by one, those who had reserved their spot would get the chance to read their work for an allotted three minutes.

After, the industry professionals would give quick feedback, no holds barred, and then move on to the next person who was brave enough to read.

We decided to give it a go.

I got up. I read the prologue for *Heir of Autumn.*

Giles and I got two requests for submission from that group of judges, and it freakin' made our day. After the Read and Critique broke, the moderator—a volunteer who kept the show on track—stopped us in the hallway as we were leaving.

"I just wanted to let you know that your piece was phenomenal. I tell you, when you started reading, the whole room got quiet, and they all leaned forward in their chairs. When I saw that, I knew you had something. Good luck at the conference, guys!"

We took our fledgling chapters to pitch after pitch, and

picked up request after request for submission, but the whale had yet to be landed. There was one industry professional whose attention I'd wanted more than any other.

Donald Maass of The Donald Maass Literary Agency was at the conference.

The previous year, I'd pitched to, gotten a submission request from, and been rejected by Jennifer Jackson, an agent who worked at the Maass Agency.

This time, I wanted to pitch to Donald. This would be the big one.

Donald was the keynote speaker at the conference, but he was not available for any pitch sessions. When I mentioned this to Chris Mandeville, one of my newest friends and one of the volunteers working the registration desk, she leaned close, looked both ways, and said, "He's not taking pitches, but I can get you a seat next to him at lunch."

"Really?" I said.

"Sure. I can let you in five minutes early. Don't be late. And don't tell anyone."

"You got it."

So when the banquet room opened for lunch, Giles and I were there, sitting on either side of Donald's placard at the table. Donald would later say that, when he sat down, he saw the ambush prepared for him, and he couldn't have been more cynical.

After opening pleasantries, I took the lead and oh so casually (I thought) steered the conversation to where both Giles and I wanted it to go.

"So I noticed you aren't doing any pitch sessions at the conference," I said between salad bites. "Do you not take pitches at conferences?"

"I usually do," Donald said. "I'm not sure why they didn't put me in any pitch sessions."

My heart began to race. "Really?"

"Yeah."

"So you're not adverse to pitches?"

"No, but pitches aren't really a good way to determine

whether or not someone is a good writer or has a good story."

My heart sank a little. "No?"

"No. I really need to see the writing."

"The writing."

"Yeah, the first chapter, maybe the first three. After I read those, I know everything I need to know. They're better than a pitch."

"You prefer to read the work."

"Yeah." He drew the word out, as though he saw through me.

I gave my best charming grin, and said with a laugh in my voice, as though I was half-joking, "So if I gave you a chapter right now, you could tell whether or not it was worth taking a look at?"

His smile tightened a little, like I'd cornered him. Which, of course, I had. He hesitated, and I wondered if he was going to shoot me down right then and there.

"Sure," he said. He made a little gesture with his hand, as though to say: Hand 'em over.

I pulled the prologue from my folder—Giles and I each had copies, just in case—and pushed them across the table. The rest of the attendees at Donald Maass's lunch table were all wide-eyed. If we'd been in a cartoon, they'd have all had open mouths. It was ballsy. I was *definitely* breaking etiquette. The lunches were for questions and socializing. They weren't for cornering agents and pitching to them. I think the other attendees thought I was going to get smacked down and possibly kicked out of the conference. Seeing Donald be receptive shocked everyone, I think.

Of course, I'd only won Round 1. The game hadn't really begun. There was plenty of time for Donald to shoot us down.

As he picked up the pages, my heart climbed into my throat. Even I knew that the mood of the editor or agent reading your pages had an effect on whether or not they reacted favorably, and I'd put him on the spot. If he wanted to smack me down without seeming like a jerk, all he really needed to do was give the first paragraph a token skim, then hand the prologue back and say, "Thanks, but it's not ready. Revise and resubmit."

That was pretty much what I expected, but writing book after book and never taking a chance hadn't brought The Dream any closer. I had to take chances somewhere or my career was going nowhere.

I waited for him to read the first few sentences, stop, and hand it back.

I watched his eyes flick from left to right, left to right as he read the whole page.

He turned the page, and continued onto the second.

Hope began to rise inside me.

He turned to read the third and final page. He tapped the pages together, laid them flat on the table, and pushed them back toward me.

"That's very good." The annoyed-yet-indulgent tone had left his voice. He was all business now, and did I detect a hint of excitement? "Is it finished?"

We had 12 chapters out of 60.

I hesitated. I desperately wanted to glance at Giles for some kind of affirmation before continuing, but I didn't dare. Any fumbling at this point would be seen as—

"Yeah," I lied. "It's finished."

"I'd like to see it." He slid his card across the table, left it where it touched the pages. Again, he looked serious. It was like he'd come to the conference to find something magical and, against all odds, that "something" might be Giles and me.

"Absolutely," I said. "We'll send it right away."

At a conference where Donald Maass, the best fantasy agent in the business, wasn't even taking story pitches, we'd pitched him and gotten a request for submission.

They hadn't even served the entree yet and already Giles and I had already hit a fucking home run. I could barely contain myself. I wanted to leap up and do a victory dance right there.

I didn't.

Instead, Giles and I both invited anyone else who wanted

to sit next to Donald and talk to him to do so. It was hard to hear when talking across the table, and we felt no desire to dominate his time now that he'd told us the best news we could possibly hear.

We only had one problem. I'd told Donald it was done. He was expecting the manuscript right after the conference.

Once the lunch ended, Giles and I took a moment to dance around like fools before we got down to brainstorming how to stall for time.

Fate served up the answer almost immediately. That afternoon, Donald debuted his new workshop "The Fire in Fiction" and, of course, Giles and I were in attendance. It was a wonderful workshop, full of inspiration, and we both drank it in.

Afterwards, we stopped Donald in the hall just long enough to say, "Fantastic workshop. That was amazing!"

"Thank you," he said.

"Hey, you said something toward the end that inspired both Giles and me."

"Oh, good," he said.

"We totally took it to heart, and it made us want to change the end of the book."

"Oh, okay."

"Could we have a few more months before we send you the manuscript? It's really going to change the ending." Which was true. We did decide to change the ending based on what Donald had said.

It was just that the ending hadn't been written yet.

"Absolutely. Take as much time as you want."

"We'll get it to you by August 1st," I promised. That gave us three months. We could do this in three months.

Couldn't we?

12

COLD PRODUCT

As it turned out, we could.

With a flurry of hard work, arguments, brilliant inspiration, arguments, more hard work, looking fretfully at the calendar, arguments, more hard work, and finally clean draft, we got the manuscript to Donald by August 1st.

Over the next month, I tried to forget all about our golden little manuscript that had sailed out into the world. I tried to reset my expectations to zero.

Yes, we'd gotten a request for submission. Yes, we'd banged out what Giles and I felt was the best novel either of us had written. Yes, we had the best fantasy agent in the biz waiting for our manuscript.

But it was only a request for submission. I'd been rejected more than a dozen times that way already.

It was early September when I received the voice message from Donald Maass.

Back in 2004, I didn't have a cell phone, nor was voicemail ubiquitous at that moment. Instead, we had a little plastic machine that picked up the land line, gave the outgoing message, and recorded the incoming message right there. You could tell that someone had called by the blinking red button on top.

I came home from work at the Juvenile Diabetes Research Foundation that afternoon and found the red button blinking, urging me to press play. So I did. It said:

"Hi Todd, this is Don Maass. I tried your work number but couldn't get through. I wanted to get you on the phone to talk about *Heir of Autumn*, which I think is absolutely, stunningly fantastic. Please call me when you get this. Okay. I'll talk to you soon."

I know the message went exactly like that because I kept the recording. In fact, I duplicated the recording on a little handheld voice recorder. And later, when mp3 files were easy to make and easy to store, I re-recorded it and kept it on my computer.

When we returned to PPWC the following year as guest instructors who had "made it," I played that recording for the audience of our "The Journey of a First Published Novel" class. At one specific point in the recording, I would rewind half a second and replay it. Several times.

"…absolutely, stunningly fantastic…"

fzzzwzzzt

"…absolutely, stunningly fantastic…"

fzzzwzzt

"…absolutely, stunningly fantastic…"

It is still on my computer. I play it whenever I'm feeling low.

Donald took that manuscript and auctioned it to the Big Seven publishers in New York City. HarperCollins bought it for $26,000/book and a three-book contract.

We got half up front, and I put new windows in my hundred-year-old fixer-upper house.

Giles and I were officially "breakout novelists." We both saw it as the beginning of our incredible journey to the top, the beginning of The Dream.

Upon our return to PPWC, we were hailed as heroes,

though it was still a full year before our debut novel was slated for publication.

But this chapter isn't about success. It's about failure.

"Failure is my teacher. Success is just the diploma."

-Howard Tayler (Writer, Illustrator)

I love that quote, because failure is where all the work happens, where all the hard decisions are made. Someone who can thrive amidst failure is indestructible. They can do anything, because what do they have to fear?

But try telling that to a thirty-something author who thought all his dreams were about to come true.

Here's what happened:

Heir of Autumn came out to mixed reviews. Publishers Weekly was lukewarm at best about Giles' and my best novel ever.

The print run for the first book of the trilogy did not sell out.

Neither did the second.

This is what is called "not selling to expectation" by the industry. HarperCollins only published the third in the series because they were contractually obligated to do so. It came out in hardback, but not in paperback, as the contract did not hold them to that.

Because the novels did not sell to expectation, they lost faith in the story. They did not offer a follow-up contract for me and Giles together, nor for Giles or me individually.

In short, we were cold product. They cut us loose.

Our rising-star careers, which began with such fanfare in 2006 with *Heir of Autumn*... sputtered and died by 2008.

In addition, the creative process with Giles had taken a dark turn. We fought even more during the second book, *Mistress of Winter*. We threw accusations like dirt clods. Attitudes soured. By the time *Queen of Oblivion*, the third and final book, was quietly released and even more quietly forgotten, we had gone our separate ways as creative partners.

13

CONFIDENCE

CONFIDENCE IS A HALLMARK WORD when it comes to writers. Yes, we're generally known as neurotic introverts who don't seem to have the confidence to even talk to new people.

But dig a little deeper and you find something different.

I mean, it takes a lot of chutzpah to write stories. It is almost inherently arrogant to think that one's writing deserves to be read. A lot of people can write stuff down. Fewer can make it interesting. Even fewer can captivate and transport their readers to another time, another place, into the head of another person.

When you're a novelist, that's exactly what you're telling people you can do. You're asking them to take their valuable time and give it to you, and you're promising that it won't be wasted.

There may be a narcissistic streak in every single writer who's ever put fingers to keyboard, but there's a flip side to that bravado that plagues writers constantly. I spend most of my time wondering if I'm any good at all. Impostor Syndrome can cut you out at the knees at any time, for any reason.

So I was devastated in the aftermath of *Heir of Autumn*, even moreso by the creative breakup between Giles and me. We'd been best friends since high school, through college, through post-college adventuring, and through this entire adventure into the publishing world.

We wouldn't be collaborating again any time soon because of how the *Heartstone Trilogy* turned out, but that wasn't the worst of it. The entire grisly process took a heavy toll on our friendship. We didn't trust each other anymore. Too much had been said to go back to the way we were.

We took a break from each other. The break turned into weeks, then to months, and then…

Giles moved away to North Carolina. It was tragic, and it was a relief at the same time. We were still both pretty numb from that experience, and the old magic simply wasn't there. After all, our enthusiasm had stemmed from being brothers-in-arms, comrades, intrepid adventurers willing to risk life and limb to road trip across the country.

Now we were married. We were fathers with all the responsibilities that come along with being fathers. The landscape had changed. I think we both thought we could continue our adventures together through parenthood and beyond. Maybe we wouldn't be road-tripping across the country, but we could ride through fantasy lands with our stories, but that path was now a blackened, smoking ruin.

We didn't reconnect for years.

This affected my writing. I'd always written my own stuff, even when collaborating with Giles, but I had always had him to fall back on, also. He was always a sounding board and someone who believed in me no matter what.

And let's face it, it wasn't one of my solo novels that had captured the attention of the big agent and been auctioned off to the Big Seven. It was a novel we wrote together.

The beginning of the *Heartstone Trilogy* had started as a euphoric ride on the clouds that I thought would define the rest of my writing career. Suddenly, that euphoria had flipped, and if the *Heartstone Trilogy* was a bellwether for the rest of my career, it was foreboding and not exciting at all.

I'd been pitched back into the mud, down with the other aspiring authors who were starting from scratch, except this was worse. I wasn't just an untested quantity, a gamble to take a chance upon. I was a proven failure.

The demons clamored in the back of my mind, and the phrase they loved best was:

"You're nothing without Giles. He's the genius and you're the workhorse. You're never going to make it without him."

I believed this to be true, but not all parts of my personality jump on bandwagons.

The Little Rebel wasn't on board.

"Fuck that," he said. "Fuck anyone who says that about you. Write your stories and let other people decide whether it's good."

The Little Rebel is dangerous, it's true. He's rude and sometimes unfair, but if it wasn't for him, my writing career might have ended right there.

The Little Rebel didn't care that I was sad. He didn't care about Giles or the big publishers or even the readers. He just kept shouting the F-word until I got back to work.

So I did. I sent Donald Maass an early version of what would later become *Fairmist*, book 1 of *The Whisper Prince Trilogy*. He liked the book, but he wasn't over-the-moon about it. He shopped it around, but didn't put it up for auction.

It didn't find a home.

I got nearly a dozen rejection letters. The one that sticks in my mind was:

"This is very well written, but we already have a series with demons. It's just not going to work for us at this time, but feel free to send us your next project."

My one thin hope had been that the publishing industry might banish my fears. I mean, if the editor of a big publisher signed me, it would mean I could write great books without Giles, right? And if they believed it, I could believe it, too.

They didn't. My personal demons swarmed me, and I lost the battle.

It would be seven years before I took another run at the hill.

I retreated to my safety zone: production in the shadows. It cost little skin to write without submitting, to go back to honing my craft until no one could deny how good it was. So that's what I did. I only showed my manuscripts to my closest friends.

It was a long journey back to the light, because finding my confidence wasn't a quick fix. I'd been attached to Giles for most of my adult life. Having to recover and build up a new way of looking at the world, a world without him, was more than a weekend project.

But I wasn't the only one going through transformation. It was 2008, and the publishing world was about to get turned on its ear. Amazon was rising, and nothing was going to be the same. Opportunities were coming, if one was willing to grab them.

The Little Rebel was about to have a lot of work to do.

14

RISING AGAIN

I NURSED MY CONFIDENCE, spending a lot of time on *Fairmist*, even though it had gotten roundly rejected. I changed the demons to "slinks," a word of my own making, though the creatures themselves were relatively the same. It bothered me that an editor could turn my book aside because of some perceived connection to another book.

I moved on from the Juvenile Diabetes Research Foundation to the American Diabetes Association, taking another promotion and continuing to raise money to fight that horrible disease.

Through connections at the ADA, I stumbled backward into another connection to the publishing industry. One of the sponsors I worked with at the ADA was married to a literary agent. He was good friends with Tom Doherty and the Doherty family, which owned Tor Books.

We started talking, and suddenly I had another line into the publishing industry.

I was still working on *Fairmist*, but I'd also begun a jaunty little project at the behest of my daughter.

At ages eight and six, my children were still sleeping in the same room, and I began to tell them stories at night.

It started as a way to make them go to sleep. One day when I came home from work, Lara looked ready to spit nails. She summarily announced that I was responsible for putting the kids to bed that night. She was tired of trying to get them to go to sleep; she was done, and now it was my turn.

I said, "Sure. No problem."

I mean, my day job was to bring complex fundraising events to the finish line, events that raised millions of dollars. I stewarded board members and I secured sponsors.

I could get a couple of kids to go to sleep.

It was all about firmness, I told myself. It was about taking a firm hold of the situation and letting them know who was in charge.

I marched into their room, where they were throwing things back and forth at each other from their beds, and I gave them my best baritone voice.

"Enough! Enough of this horsing around!"

They looked up at me with big, wide eyes, and they stopped throwing things. See? Kids respond to a big, baritone voice.

"Good. That's good. Now," I said. "Go to sleep."

They looked at each other, then at me.

And they burst into laughter.

The toys began flying back and forth. I blinked and had the sudden, sinking feeling that I was in over my head.

What was I going to do to make them go to sleep? I'd tried the deep voice thing. I could shift into full terror mode and scream at them, but I didn't believe in that type of parenting. I wasn't going to spank them. What arrow did I have left in my quiver that was going to be able to hit this bullseye—

Say...

"Who wants to hear a story?" I asked.

The toys stopped flying. The kids looked at me.

"What kind of story?" Elo wanted to know.

"The kind I make up right here, right now, just for you."

Dash narrowed his eyes, alert for some trick. "You're going to make it up?"

"Right here, right now."

"Yes!" Elo said.

"Okay," Dash said.

"Can we make it up with you?" Elo wanted to know.

"If you quiet down. But first you have to get completely ready to sleep. Sleeping clothes on. Covers up to your chins, and we're going to turn the light off."

"Night lights too?" Dash asked.

"Night lights can stay on."

They settled down into their beds.

I told the story of Hugo the Turtle. Hugo was a turtle who lived by a reedy lake. At night, he turned himself upside down and slept in a dent in the ground that perfectly fit his shell.

Hugo was boring by design, as boring as I could make him. Everything he did, he did verrrry slowwwly.

I blathered on about Hugo and his painfully ordinary tasks. Walking down to the lake. Walking back. Getting water from the lake. Walking back. Eating his dinner. Walking back. Everything took him a long time to do. The kids loved Hugo, and he put them right to sleep.

That first night, I felt utterly brilliant.

The second night, I was happy the plan had worked.

The third night, I did my duty, drawling out the boring story, eager for it to end.

The fourth night, I fell asleep before the kids.

The fifth night, the boredom was absolutely killing me. I simply couldn't stick to it.

Yes, it put the kids to sleep, but I was going out of my mind. After a week or so of this, I couldn't take it anymore. I introduced a new character into the mix: Hugo's adventurous friend, Gruffy the Griffon.

Pip and Squeak soon followed as Gruffy's companions, and Hugo was left behind at the little lake.

Gruffy was a young and noble griffon who would do anything for his friends. Pip was the mother-friend, a toucan who repeated everything he said twice in a high-pitched voice. Squeak was a mouse who only ever said one word: "Squeak!"

Gruffy and Pip always replied to Squeak in a way that showed the kids that they could understand Squeak's comments as though he'd spoken in English. The children had to infer from context what the mouse was saying.

Of course, I soon completely lost the main purpose of the storytelling. The kids wanted to stay up late to hear more adventures of Gruffy, Pip, and Squeak.

And frankly, so did I.

It was an unforgettable time of bonding with my kids, but it didn't become relevant until two years later when Elo had moved into her own room. One night when I was tucking her in, she said, "Dad, you write books."

It was a statement, not a question.

"Yeah," I said.

"Why don't you write the Gruffy book?"

"Hmmm."

Because I made it up on the spot, and it's utterly simplistic, I thought, but I didn't want to yuck her yum.

"It's a great bed time story, sweetie. But I don't know that it would make a good book."

"Why not?"

"Because..." I began, but I didn't finish that thought. "I... I don't know. Do you really think it would be a good book?"

"My friends would love that story, daddy. You should do it. It's a good story."

"Hmmm. I'll think about it."

"Think about it a lot, daddy. People would love that story."

The idea took hold. I figured I'd give it a shot, but it didn't come easy. I had a devil of a time trying to find the beginning of that book. I hacked and wrangled and hacked and wrangled. The solution finally came when I decided to put Elowyn, remade as a character named Lorelei, into the protagonist's spot.

That changed everything.

Before, I'd been trying to chronicle the exact story I'd told them as a bedtime story. Now, though, it had an entirely new life. Lorelei was the bridge between that oral bedtime story and the page.

Once I had her, the book flew along.

I had just finished the book when I met Bill Golliher, who would become my new agent. He loved it, and he took it to Kathleen Doherty, the publisher at Tor.

In the fall of 2014, I had another publishing contract.

The publishing landscape had begun to change by then. Amazon had hit the scene with Kindle years before. The big publishers had dismissed e-books as a fad at first, secure in their dominance as they had been for a century. But e-books were turning into a reading revolution and a sales juggernaut. People loved it.

Far too late, the big publishers seemed to wake up. They became combative as they realized just how much of a threat Amazon was becoming. I remember hearing about meetings that the big publishers had with Amazon, where they were, I think, trying to induct Amazon into this club of publishers and force them to play by rules that had been set in stone decades ago.

Amazon, of course, had no interest. The big publishers had nothing to tempt them except the status quo, and Amazon wanted a revolution. They'd created a market unlike any other, and they wanted it to stretch from horizon to horizon. They wanted *all* the market share, not just the share that the big publishers wanted to give them.

Kindle Direct Publishing (KDP) appeared almost immediately—a way for indie authors to publish their e-books. With a manuscript, a cover, and a modicum of design skill, a writer could publish their book in an afternoon. CreateSpace followed, Amazon's hard copy indie publishing arm. With a bit more interior design skill, those same indie writers could have a published paperback in their hands in six weeks! Amazon gave every single would-be author the opportunity to have at least a part of The Dream: a published novel.

Suddenly anyone—literally anyone—could publish their

work. Whether you were a retired teacher who had always wanted to write a book or a teenager fresh out of high school who wanted to be the next Stephen King, you now had a place to publish. In short Amazon had, with one swift stroke, removed all the gatekeepers.

Before Amazon created KDP and CreateSpace, there weren't many avenues for indie authors to publish without going through those gatekeepers of big publishing. The entire business side of writers conferences were centered around courting those gatekeepers.

Once, indie publishing was called "vanity publishing," and it meant you paid a small press to publish your book. You paid someone to edit it, or edited it yourself, and coughed up $10,000 to do a print run.

Before 2015, if you printed your books through a "vanity press," no one else in the industry would take you seriously. Independent bookstores would rarely take your books, and big chains like Barnes and Noble would shun you. Most authors considered vanity press authors to be the rock bottom of the talent set.

Before the Amazon revolution, I'd seen a few authors who'd printed through vanity presses, and they literally could not *give* their books away. At a folk fest in Lyons, CO, I remember seeing one of these authors handing out free copies of his book to people as they headed to the folk fest. Most of them ended up in the garbage.

KDP and CreateSpace changed that perception. It started slowly. At first, there was an inclination to treat authors who were published through KDP the same as authors who'd paid vanity presses to print their books.

But something different happened with KDP. Those authors began to make money. As it turned out, readers didn't much care what publishers—or "serious" authors—thought about the books they read. With Amazon's wild west platform where anyone could potentially see any kind of book, the readers made their own decisions. There was no distribution bottleneck.

Entrenched institutions tend to change slowly, and all of us authors who had been following what would later be called the "traditional" or "trad" publishing path, myself included, looked at this indie opportunity as something to shrug at curiously.

I still wanted The Dream. I wanted to have a big publisher pick up my book, call me and tell me that they wanted to make me the next Big Author and offer me a $250,000 advance.

No way was that happening if I just slapped my story up on KDP.

But I began to feel the changes in the trad publishing industry as I navigated it for the second time. They were already feeling the sting from the success of KDP-published indie authors. Advances for contracted books were lower across the board, unless you were already a literary giant that could bring in the big money, like the James Pattersons and the Stephen Kings.

The big publishers didn't control the entire publishing landscape anymore; they couldn't risk pouring money into new author gambles as readily, or not nearly as much money, anyway. Amazon was breathing down their necks, shrinking their market share, diminishing their dominance. The big publishers didn't seem interested in cultivating new authors as much as they wanted a sure thing. They would go so far as to "throw this novel at the wall and see if it sticks," see if it makes money right out of the gate. But there was no indication that they were interested in the long haul with a new author.

And it showed in the advance I was offered.

The last time I'd been courted by a big publisher, Giles and I had received a three-book contract with $26,000 per book.

This time, they offered me $7,000 for *The Wishing World* (the Gruffy book), and a one-book contract.

I was so disappointed that I asked to have a call directly with the publisher. I mean, I saw *The Wishing World* as my breakout novel, and I was on the verge of pulling the project, taking it somewhere else. I desperately wanted to be published with Tor, but $7,000 was practically nothing. It certainly wasn't going to pay my bills until my next novel. And that was all I would get for years. The traditional publishing model was to acquire a book and publish it no sooner than a year later. Usually it was closer to two. $7,000 was supposed to last me that entire span?

It was a token. I wanted to know if they really believed in this story or if they were just collecting the rights for little projects and, if one of them were to somehow skyrocket, they'd get 90% of whatever it made.

I actually got the publisher on the phone to talk to me, and I essentially said (though not in these words, but ones far more diplomatic):

"$7,000? What the hell? If you don't believe in this book, just say so, and I'll sell it somewhere else."

They said (in almost exactly these words):

"Don't take the size of the advance to reflect how much faith we have in this book. We love *The Wishing World*."

That pacified me, because I *wanted* to believe those words. That's what I wanted to hear. I didn't really care if the money came after the publishing or before, only that it came. Only that *The Wishing World* got the full support of the publisher because they believed in it like I believed in it.

My confidence in my own writing was wrapped up in what the publisher believed. Their faith in the book was more important than the advance. I could take the hit at the start. My emotional need outweighed my financial need.

I also knew that if the publisher believed in the story, they would more avidly push it. That was the most important for its overall success. So I agreed. I took the $7,000.

I learned a valuable lesson in the subsequent months, a lesson that has tripped up the ignorant for as long as the human race has had the power of speech.

Talk is cheap. It costs very little to tell an author what they want to hear, because we *want* to hear it. We want The Dream, and they know it.

In truth, the advance *does* indicate how much faith the publisher has in the story. It indicates exactly that. Of course it does. At the very least, it illustrates how much the publisher is going to back the project, especially if it gets rocky.

You put $1,000,000 into something, you fight for it. It's good business sense. You have to protect your investment.

You put $7,000 into something, who cares? If it doesn't hit, write it off. Move on.

Being a small business owner myself these days, I completely understand. If I have something that is losing money, I don't put more money into it. I get rid of it. I have to, or my business goes under. So I get it.

I just didn't get it back then. The Dream was large in my head, and I was willing to believe whatever anybody told me as long as I could continue believing. I was poised for success, but I was headed for another failure. I was about to learn so many things, but I was going to slip once more. I was going to get one finger on The Dream and then watch it fall away again.

I'll get back to that in a couple of chapters.

For now, let me state for the record: Tor was wonderful to me. One of my favorite moments was flying out to meet them. Tom Doherty himself took us all to lunch. I got to see his office, take a picture with him there. By the way, it's in the Flatiron Building. For those of you Marvel nuts (like me), that's the building that houses the Daily Bugle in the Tobey Maguire Spiderman movies. Remember the office in which J. Jonah Jameson harangued people? Yeah, that's Tom Doherty's office. And I got to stand there and look out over the city right next to that fantasy publishing legend.

Tor did make one of my dreams come true: to be published by the premier fantasy publisher, Tor. Just my name, and not a co-author credit. In the end, it *did* give me back my confidence.

But it also cleared away some of the fog around The Dream. One of my fondest hopes was that someone was going to "discover me," promote me, and pay me truckloads of money. That was an illusion.

No one was going to make The Dream come true for me. People in the publishing industry, whether trad or indie, are not there to make my dreams come true. They're there to make their own dreams come true. We will share common goals. We can even elevate one another. We can be generous and pay kindness forward.

But you are not the protagonist of their story. They are.

I needed to make my own dream come true. And that crossroads was fast approaching. I was about to face my hardest choice yet.

One of my favorite lines comes from a Rush song named *Freewill*. It is:

"If you choose not to decide, you still have made a choice."

The Universe was just about done with my dithering. The cliff was near. The invisible wall was moving.

She was about to force my hand.

15

COMMITMENT

Let's talk about commitment.

Boy. This is a loaded word for me. Not only does it have different levels of importance to different people, but there are different levels of meaning just within the freaking word itself.

You can be committed to brushing your teeth twice a day. Simple. A good idea. If you miss a few times, who cares? The sky ain't going to fall. Catch it the next time around, and you're fine.

You can be committed to getting your homework done for class or to getting to your job on time. If you miss a time or two, you could see a drop in your grades or get harangued by your boss. And that's a little painful. Nobody wants their grades to drop; nobody wants to get harangued by the boss. But you'll live (the Little Rebel might even *like* it).

You can be committed to staying faithful to your spouse. If you miss a time or two on that… Well, that's a whole different kettle of fish, isn't it? That could trigger horrible situations. The hatred of a spouse. Revenge. Despair. The collapse of your family unit, of your finances. A boiled rabbit on the stove. You get my point.

I'd been committed to my writing career my entire life. But it started out a toothbrush commitment, and it rose to maybe the level of a homework commitment. It was something I felt I should do. It was something I felt if I kept doing, things would pan out for me. The Dream would finally visit me, finally become my reality.

That's the way I looked at it up to my critical moment, my "planting my flag in the hill" moment.

To tell that story, I have to rewind four years to 2010, because that's when the seeds of this decision got planted. They hadn't started sprouting yet, but they were there, nestled in the soil.

A more subtle version of that "my body is flying apart" feeling had begun inside me. It wasn't nearly so obvious or violent as it had been in my nightmare so long ago, but I felt a sense of foreboding. It was like my normal skin had been shifted a quarter inch to the left and I couldn't get it to fit right anymore. It made me want to move, to shake free. It made me feel like I was in the wrong place all the time.

I'd felt something like this over and over in my life. I'm probably not the only one. It always precipitated a change for me: a move from one city to another, quitting a job, starting on a road trip, that kind of thing.

At this stage in my life—married, two kids, responsible job—some might say it was "the seven-year itch," that claustrophobic feeling that family men sometimes get when they realized they've committed to not just a wife and domestication, but to kids as well. They suddenly wake up and see that the next twenty years of their lives are locked down, and each day will closely resemble the day before. That's the closest parallel I can get to describe the feeling, though this itch had nothing to do with my family.

It had everything to do with my day job.

Family-wise, I loved my wife. I loved my kids. I loved being a husband and a father, and I had no intention of leaving them. That had been done to me, and the Little Rebel was adamant that I would never, ever do that. I would rather die first.

Nope. This agitated feeling had come for me before. This "something is off" feeling had driven me from high school and made me skip college for three years. This same feeling had blasted me out of Colorado Springs the very moment I graduated college, forced me to find out what was next rather than hanging around in a place where I'd been comfortable, credible, loved. This feeling had pushed me to New York City, and it had pushed me out when it was time.

In short, this feeling was the Universe warning me of a crossroads. I wasn't building the ideal life I dreamed about, and the invisible wall was coming. After it reached me, nothing would ever be the same.

My emotional state had all the ear-marks of a mid-life crisis. Hell, maybe it was one. I was the right age. Those start around forty, right?

But this crossroads had been in my future since I was eighteen years old and began writing that first novel.

Slowly, the crossroads came into focus. I wasn't living my worst life. Goodness knows, so many things were going right for me. Not many people get as lucky as I did in my spouse, in my children, in my finances. We weren't rich, but we had enough to eat and a roof over our heads. My children had known stability all their lives, something even I couldn't claim as a child. So it wasn't that I was living a bad life...

I just wasn't living my ideal life.

I was living a life halfway the way I envisioned. I'd taken runs at the hill here and there. I'd experimented. I'd ridden the carousel, but I'd never fully committing to trying for the brass ring.

My day job hadn't been just a day job for quite some time now, and I wasn't even sure when it had switched over. It became crystal clear, though, when one of my best friends from college, Megan, and I were talking on the phone. I made some offhand comment like...

"I feel stuck. I just wonder when my career is really going

to start." I was, of course, referring to my writing career.

"Honey, you've already got a career," she said.

"I do?" I asked, literally not knowing what she meant. I think I was kind of hoping she'd stroke my ego and talk about all the stories I'd had published.

"Duh! You're the Director of Development at the American Diabetes Association, baby. That's a real job. That *is* your career."

Another person might have glowed at that. I mean, being the Director of Development at a well-established, well-respected, nationwide nonprofit like the ADA is the kind of job people vie for. It's the kind of job you go to college specifically to get.

And here I was. Not only doing that job and doing it well, but I had opportunities to go even higher. A regional position. Perhaps even a national position. Hell, if I set my sights for it, I could aspire to be the CEO of the whole damned organization someday. It should have lit me up with pride.

Instead, the words felt like a gut punch.

The truth of them sank in. In college, my close-knit group of friends talked a lot about following our dreams. We made fun of those who settled for an ordinary life instead of going after the thing they most wanted.

And here I was. Megan was right. I'd spent thirteen years in the nonprofit sector. I was a fundraising professional. That was a solid, well-paying, well-respected career doing something that *mattered*. I should have been proud. I should have clapped myself on the back for my hard work and my good choices.

But I felt ill. I felt the crossroads was in front of me, and my opportunity to choose was slowly slipping away.

The writing was calling me. *That's* why my skin didn't feel like it fit quite right.

I'm not the only one who feels this itch. Writers are called to write. Oftentimes, we don't know how—or when—it's supposed to happen, but we are called. Not everyone answers the call. Some answer, experience failure, and then hide from that excruciating pain.

Some never try, just assuming that writing for a living is a ridiculous proposition, so they sputter out a few pieces as a hobby, and sometimes daydream about what life might be like if they were a successful writer.

Some go after it, moving from job to job, living in poverty—or at the good graces of a spouse or patron who foots the bill for them—and try with everything they have.

But all writers feel the call. And I was running out of time. It plagued me. As I approached my fortieth birthday, I began to get depressed. After a few days of this, Lara noticed.

"You okay?" she asked.

"I'm in a funk," I said. "This same thing happened to me when I was twenty-nine. Remember my Thirty-Year-Old Letter?"

When I was thirty, I'd sent out a self-reflective email to all of my friends, my reaction to the "end of a decade." An assessment of where I was in life.

"I remember."

"Well, it's another decade down. I'm almost forty, and I haven't *done* anything yet."

My wife—my wonderful, beautiful wife—absorbed that statement, held me, and whispered words of encouragement. I rose the next day and went to my job, still agitated, still uncomfortable, still unsure of what to do.

Lara got up the next morning and got to work. She made a series of calls, sent out emails, and typed texts that culminated in the creation of what is now my most prized possession (and this is coming from a guy who owns a genuine replica of Schwartzenegger's Conan the Barbarian sword. Just sayin').

She took that statement, reached out to all of my friends and family and asked them how they'd respond if I'd said that to them.

From their replies, she created a hand-bound book filled with pictures from my past, drawings from the kids, their specific response to my statement "I haven't done anything yet," and their predictions for my future.

She painted "The Book of Todd: 40th Edition" on the

front cover and gave it to me at my fortieth birthday party.

That incredible gift brought me to tears. There were so many beautiful things said on those pages, so many wonderful adventures photographed and recalled. If there was anything that could have made me feel better about my life, it had to be this.

But it didn't. It only heightened the feeling that had been making the back of my neck itch, because it illustrated to me that in the past, I had almost always made that rarer choice. I had chosen adventure, intuition, the crazy path, and it had worked out for me again and again.

Yet now I was choosing the safe path, the path I could see the end of, or at least predict the end of. One of the inscriptions in the book rang in my ears. It was:

"I do believe Todd is (not will be) a successful writer…"

This was written by Jim Swayze, a friend I'd made during my JDRF days. He was the CEO of a regional healthcare company, a man of high community standing, philanthropic disposition, and sizable wealth. I never really understood why he'd wanted to be friends with me, but I cherished the connection.

He was also an avid science fiction and fantasy reader, and he had been consistently supportive of my writing. I always felt he believed I'd make it some day.

But to have him say that he thought I'd *already* made it, well… I couldn't actually hear those words. I couldn't believe them. To me, being successful meant having The Dream. The fame. The money. I couldn't possibly believe that I was successful at writing if I wasn't making my living at it. Hell, I couldn't even support *myself* with the pittance I made from my written words, let alone make some kind of replacement income for the day-job-career that now held me tightly in its fist.

It was nice to hear all those kind words, but it only made me want to wriggle out of my skin all the more.

I loved my fortieth birthday, but the next morning I felt off, dissatisfied, trapped.

I went back to my day job for the next three years and day by day, it began to pale.

By the end of those years, I hated going to work. I mean, I loved the people. I loved the volunteers. I even enjoyed some of the work, but a chasm was growing in my chest.

By 2013, I'd been Director of Development for four years. I'd passed up a couple opportunities to apply to become an Executive Director in another state, but it was becoming obvious to not only me, but also to my boss, that I was stagnating.

And the Universe finally took the choice away from me.

My crossroads began at my yearly evaluation. My boss said I'd seemed a little off, and she asked me to open up.

"No repercussions," she said. "Tell me what you're thinking."

After a long hesitation where my cautionary voice reminded me that you should never *ever* tell your boss that you don't really want to be doing your job. You just don't say that, even if that's what you feel. You smile and say something—anything—else. Especially when you're in a prestigious, sought-after position with a high salary cap.

"What am I thinking?" I blurted. "I'm thinking I should be an author, not a Director of Development or Executive Director or anything of that kind. I don't want to be a nonprofit fundraiser anymore."

She made sympathetic noises and then we talked about goals for the job. She said no repercussions, but from that moment forward, her demeanor toward me changed. I was no longer "her guy." She began giving responsibilities to other people. She began seeing my work in a different light. Any victories I had were not celebrated. Any mistakes I made were highlighted.

In short, she wanted me gone. She wanted my high salary back in the salary pool. She wanted me to move on to the next phase of my career, wherever or whatever that may be.

During the day, I felt that sinking feeling as I watched her turn away from me. At night, I lay in torture thinking about how I had completely shot myself in the foot. My family's entire financial stability depended on what I earned at the ADA, and I'd sabotaged it.

There was no choice now; I had to move on. The only possible way I could stay with the ADA organization was to completely change my mind, my attitude, my heart, and dive back into my work with vigor. And even if I could do that, I'd have to move to another chapter. My boss was done with me. That meant moving out of the state, and I wasn't leaving Colorado. Uproot my family? Take away the stability I'd created for my kids? And for what? A job I didn't really want?

Now I really felt trapped, like a caged animal who didn't have any direction to leap. I mean, I could go to another nonprofit. I had a fantastic resume. I could have become the Director of Development or even Executive Director at any number of non-profits in Denver.

I applied to several and received interest.

But I didn't... want... ANY of that. No matter which way I turned, it felt like I was putting my heart in a vice and squeezing.

I'd been honest with my boss about what I wanted, but I had no idea how to make that into a career that could support my family. I simply couldn't go from making nearly six figures a year to making nothing. I couldn't. I wouldn't.

I lay in torment night after night. I skipped everything else as the transformation pulled me into its grips. We had a family reunion in South Dakota that year, an opportunity to see Mount Rushmore with my kids, and I passed. I saw the train wreck coming and I couldn't simply go on vacation and assume the train wasn't going to crash.

I had to know what my next step was.

I needed to make money. I needed to be a writer. And I couldn't see a way to marry the two.

After days of agony, my perspective pivoted, and I finally saw the path. I saw it so clearly. It was simple and dangerous. I didn't have to make a hundred thousand dollars right now. I just needed to make the decision.

I just needed to make the absolute, unequivocal, death-before-surrender commitment.

16

THE JUMP

I REMEMBER VIVIDLY LAYING IN TORMENT those two weeks my family was away as I resisted the fear and the danger of the crossroads. I wished I was in South Dakota with them, experiencing those "first times" with my children. I would later hear that a herd of buffalo had moved through their camp, and everyone had had to cluster into the buildings until the buffalo moved on. I'd missed that and so many other amazing, once-in-a-lifetime moments.

But I was undergoing transformation, and there is no pain so exquisite as resisting transformation. I knew what I wanted. I could see the first few steps of the path, but it fell quickly into shadow and turned beyond my sight. I couldn't predict where it would go. It could lead to my ideal life, or it could lead over the edge of a cliff.

I was horribly out of practice. When I was younger, I'd made a life out of charging at things that scared me. I'd honed my senses, my skills, my intuition, and it was all because of that original nightmare. By the time I settled down, I was an expert at leaping off cliffs.

But I wasn't leaping for one anymore. It wouldn't just be me that suffered from a fall. This time, I was dragging three other people with me.

I simply couldn't do that. Could I?

I stalked around the house, swinging my fists. I yelled. I knelt at my bedside clenching the covers, crying, trying to expel the overwhelming fear that frosted my insides.

I had been offered a job at the Denver Performing Arts Center. It was an amazing opportunity. I was steeped in the arts. I was a writer. An artist. I'd minored in dance in college. This was a step in the right direction, right? I'd be at the center of something that was meant to promote the arts in my home state. I'd be around the arts all the time.

But I wouldn't be an artist myself.

When I considered taking that job, I got a fluttery feeling of panic. It spooked my soul, like it knew this was my last chance to dedicate my life to storytelling. If I chose wrong, that part of my soul was going to die. I'd never see it again. No more writing euphoria. No more muse.

I would spend the rest of my life doing whatever else was left. Fundraising. Board meetings. Ladder climbing.

Two days before my family was supposed to come home, I got still. I got calm. Maybe some of my old adventure coping mechanisms returned. My back was against the wall, but I'd had my back against the wall before. When that happened, things got really simple. When your choices boiled down to one, you make that one choice.

The invisible wall was about push me off the cliff, and I'd fall and fall and fall, over and over again for the rest of my life, until I eventually died.

Or I could jump.

I was terrified I would let my family down, that the safe little home Lara and I had built would crumble away to nothing, that the fear I'd felt as a child, the uncertainty of where I was going to lay my head tonight or tomorrow night would soon be a fear my children would also know.

But the terror went even deeper than that. It wasn't just

about my family and their safety. It was more primal, something linked all the way back to my fourteen-year-old self, a boy who couldn't stop his parents' divorce, a boy who desperately wanted his father to come back after he'd left for California, a boy who thought that if he was just good enough, if he was just successful enough, if he was larger than life, his father would return. I'd given my all to being that good, that successful, that larger than life, and it hadn't worked.

What if, now, I gave my *all* to my writing, tried as hard as I could, put all of my focus, intelligence, and effort into making this life…

And I failed?

I'd excelled at every job I'd ever had, at every endeavor I'd undertaken because I wasn't afraid of failure. I wasn't afraid of failure because I hadn't cared if I failed at being a fundraiser because deep down, I didn't give a rip about being a fundraiser. My day jobs had been only tangentially connected to my soul; I'd been ready to clip free at any moment. So I didn't care if I left a day job behind me in ruin. Morgan Stanley didn't care whether I continued being a Powerpoint operator in their creative services department in New York. If I left, they'd just replace me. So I didn't put my self-worth on the line there. I went in and did my best without fear of losing my self-worth. As a result, I'd always done an excellent job. The same with JDRF. The same with the ADA.

But my soul was completely intertwined with my writing. It was my identity. I'd protected it and preserved it behind thick walls. If someone had asked me why I never made it as a writer, I could always tell them…

"Well, I had a young family at the time…"

"I was going to school at the time…"

"My job got crazy busy at that time…"

Step and repeat. There are a thousand valid and worthy excuses I could put inside those quotation marks.

But the truth was: they were all excuses.

That's what I really wrestled with for those two weeks my family was gone. That was what forced me into a corner during the last two days where I saw that the only path forward was the most terrifying.

I clenched my teeth and set to work. In those short two days between my resolution and the return of my family, I worked it out. I looked straight at the ugly fear and came up with a plan. I broke down our finances into all the component parts. I worked out the math.

I would still have to have a day job; that much was certain. I simply couldn't, in good conscience, drop my income to zero. I was going to jump, but I needed some kind of parachute to extend the fall a little. Maybe I'd crash into the ground, but I could at least give myself a little more time to figure out a way to make it work.

I had to move on from the ADA; that much was clear. My boss didn't want me there anymore, and I might actually get fired. Also, even if I reapplied myself, convinced my boss to find me useful again, I might in a moment of weakness convince myself to fall into the same old groove. There was simply too much familiarity there, too much temptation to revert to the status quo.

I had to make a break, and it needed to be a break with intention. I needed to make a statement to the world, to my friends and family, but most of all to that scared little part of my soul.

My grand gesture had to say: *I got you, little part of my soul. Don't go away yet. I'm working it out.*

I took a job as an Executive Assistant at Rose Community Foundation.

The interview process went smoothly. There was only one bump in the road when they asked me point blank:

"You were a director before. Why would you want to be an assistant?"

I told them, "I want very well-defined duties. I want to come to work for forty hours a week and then forget about the foundation when I leave. During my forty hours, I'll give you everything I've got. But my true goal is to get my writing career off the ground."

They believed my words. Probably because they were true. They hired me.

I had a plan. I did not want to be an Executive Assistant, and seeing that title beneath my name unequivocally reminded me of my true purpose. There would be no falling into a comfortable groove here.

I'd begun my journey. Finally. After feeling the call at eighteen, producing novel after novel in the shadows, I was finally planting my flag in the hill. I was going to do this. There was no hiding behind little victories in arenas that did not hold my soul.

I was putting it out there for one and all. Whether I succeeded or failed spectacularly...

I was a writer.

17

GOODBYE TO TRAD PUBLISHING

THE QUESTION WAS: HOW DO I DO IT?

I still didn't know. I'd given up my promising nonprofit career to follow a will-o-the-wisp into the forest. I still didn't know where I was going, only that I needed to move forward.

I'd grown up with the notion that the only way to be a Stephen-King-level author was to get the great agent, sign the big contract, and let the money and accolades roll in. And I had one, thin chance to make that happen still. The negotiations with Tor for *The Wishing World* had proceeded apace. Maybe I wasn't going to be the youthful prodigy anymore; I'd sailed past that horizon. I was forty-four, after all. But it could still happen.

Right about the time I left the ADA, I signed the $7,000 contract with Tor and put all my hopes on the fact that the book would break records, that the royalties would roll in, and the advance wouldn't matter anymore.

I had determined that this time was going to be different than my last trad publishing contract. Back during the *Heartstone Trilogy*, right before it was about to publish, I'd come to Giles with a hare-brained scheme to try to boost the sales.

When I was much younger, I'd watched my mother try to do Amway, a multi-level marketing company, and I tried to get Giles on board with that kind of thing.

"If we could reach out to all of our friends and family," I'd said. "And ask them to each not only buy a book, but ask ten of their friends to buy a book, and then ask each of those friends to tap three of their friends, and then possibly have each of those three friends tap one of their friends to buy a book, that could be huge for the opening."

Giles looked at me like I was making a joke.

"No, I'm serious!" I said.

"I'm not a marketer," he said. "I'm an author. That's the publisher's job."

After he said that, I immediately felt silly for suggesting it. I mean, multi-level marketing *was* lame. It had been lame for a number of years. A punchline. It would probably never have worked anyway. And he was right, wasn't he? This was trad publishing. It was the job of the author to write the story, and it was the job of the publisher to market and sell the story.

I'd let it go.

And *Heir of Autumn* hadn't sold to expectation.

I will admit my Amway-style marketing idea probably wouldn't have moved the needle. But even if it had failed on nine-out-of-ten fronts, it would have shown one thing: I was all in. I would try anything.

Once *Heir of Autumn* came out to less-than-robust sales, once the trilogy slid slowly from the limelight into the shadows, it plagued me that I hadn't done everything to make those books succeed. I hadn't fought, worked, flailed, cajoled, peddled, fallen on my face—done EVERYTHING within my power to ensure success. I'd always wondered if just a little push might have changed the outcome.

I swore to myself I'd never just sit back and do nothing again. I was not going to make the same mistake with *The Wishing World.*

So when I visited the publishers of Tor in New York City,

I brought an entire pitch on how we could promote this. I made a Powerpoint presentation, literally stood in a board room, and went through a slide-by-slide marketing idea that would include targeting thirty elementary schools in Colorado. I planned to visit each of these schools, do a workshop about creative writing, and promote *The Wishing World*. That was just to start. We could potentially do it nationwide if they wanted to fly me around and help me promote it.

They didn't go for the grandiose parts of the idea. They weren't going to fly me anywhere, but they did agree to give me a number of books to give away during the promotion in Colorado.

They also agreed to the standard things trad publishers do. They put *The Wishing World* into their catalogue and newsletters, which went out to thousands of educators.

That fall and winter, I packed up my little cart and went to schools. I was relentless. It became my passion to visit and talk and sell, visit and talk and sell. I pulled in all the favors from my American Diabetes Association and Rose Community Foundation connections.

I blew past my thirty-school goal and visited fifty-two schools in Colorado.

If you were a kid in 4th or 5th grade in the Denver area the fall of 2016, you probably knew about *The Wishing World*. My wife Lara even went to a bunch of those visits with me, and we took pictures of us with a copy of *The Wishing World* in front of each of the schools before my talks.

These efforts sold a bunch of books in my region. That fall *The Wishing World* hit #10 on the Mountains and Plains Independent Booksellers bestseller list.

Nationwide, it did practically nothing.

That showed me two things:

First, the big publishers weren't going to do more than their prescribed checklist unless I asked them, and probably not even then. More than that, maybe they didn't have the power to lift me up to stardom.

Second, and most interestingly, I *did* have the power to lift myself up. I mean, the Mountains and Plains Independent Booksellers bestseller list wasn't the New York Times bestseller list, but it was something.

And I'd done that.

It had been a grueling schedule, tons of effort, and I'd received no money for it.

But I'd moved the needle. Me.

That broke down one of largest illusions of the trad publishing paradigm: that an author couldn't do anything, couldn't get anywhere, without the help of the established publishing hierarchy.

An indie author *could* succeed.

More illusions were about to be stripped away, and a hundred more doors were about to open as well. Traditional publishing, for me, was about to fade.

The indie world was calling, and I was going to plunge in headfirst.

18

INDIE AUTHOR

LET'S TALK ABOUT THE INDIE PUBLISHING WORLD.

I mentioned the stigma of "vanity presses" before 2015. The exact time frame could be argued. But back around that time and before, "real" authors and "real" publishers looked down on anyone who was "self published." Bookstores wouldn't showcase those books. You could barely *give* them away.

But by 2016, Amazon had moved inexorably forward. Bookstores weren't the only place for readers to get their fiction fix. Traditional publishers weren't the only place for authors to print their books. And the progression of printing technology—the invention of print-on-demand—meant that an indie author didn't need to pay $10,000 on a large run of books to have a published copy.

They could pay per book.

All they needed to do was learn how to upload their books to CreateSpace, give Amazon a percentage of every copy sold, and they could have a published book in hand in a few weeks.

Revolutionary.

Being as how I'd been somewhat accepted by the traditional publishing world—having four books traditionally published was four more than most authors I knew—I'd barely explored indie publishing.

But despite my best efforts, *The Wishing World* did not sell to the level Tor wanted. And as I suspected, when the book didn't explode onto the scene, there was no follow-up of support. They didn't say, "No worries, Fahnestock. You'll get 'em next time. Sometimes it takes a while to build an audience. Let's come out with a few more in the series and see if the sales go up."

Nope. They cut bait and I drifted down the river. Again.

Let's back up seven months.

Before *The Wishing World* ever hit the market, I'd resurrected *Fairmist* and cut the manuscript down to its leanest, meanest version with the help of Chris Mandeville.

I'd loaded *Fairmist* up to CreateSpace, set up a big indie release party, and was enacting part of my Amway multi-level marketing plan, intending to drive all my friends and family to buy books from Amazon on the same day to spike the rankings.

And it worked. Sort of.

Fairmist hit #14 on the Amazon bestseller list the midnight of its release. That part succeeded. My hope was that if I could appear on the bestseller list, tons of readers would see it, be intrigued, and buy it. Then the book would lift free of the jumpstart and continue selling on its own.

That part failed.

Through whatever algorithmic rules governed Amazon at the time, my launch party sales were delayed. *Fairmist*'s spike in the rankings happened at midnight. It did not catch hold. It did not alert all fantasy fans of its potential greatness. And the next day *Fairmist* fell down the rankings almost as fast as it had risen.

Fairmist did not become my day-saver. My rankings-oriented strategy was a one-day wonder that, I think, did little to bring attention to my book or my writing.

I wasn't worried. That little foray into indie publishing was just a toe in the water. I hadn't expected it to do well, and I didn't need it to. I had an ace in the hole, after all. *The Wishing World* was coming soon, and I was still banking on the traditional publishing world to make The Dream come true.

Seven months after my indie trial with *Fairmist*, in October of 2016, *The Wishing World* was released.

In my personal life, Lara had secured a job at Denver Urban Gardens and had been thriving for a year. The two working parents thing had made it hard on the kids, but the extra income was a godsend.

It gave me the opportunity to enact a new phase of my plan. Lara wanted to work. She wanted to have her own career in the workforce, and she was happy to switch places with me as the primary breadwinner if I took the stay-at-home duties while I got my writing career off the ground.

So as we approached the release of *The Wishing World*, I was full of The Dream. Not only did I have an indie book on the market, but I was about to have a smash hit trad published book released. It seemed like everything was rising, and Lara and I both made the decision. I was going to quit my job at Rose Community Foundation and become a full-time writer at the beginning of 2017.

Over 2016 while we were both working full time, we saved up $10,000 to bolster Lara's income for the following year when I let go of my day job. This was the parachute. I hadn't known what it was going to look like when I made the decision to leave the ADA, but now here it was.

As I did school visit after school visit, I had high hopes for my writing career as we headed into the holidays.

My plan was to make $20,000 the first year from royalties of *The Wishing World* and the advance from *The Wishing World II* when Tor signed on for the next few books in the series.

The year turned. I quit my job. My last day was February 6th, 2017. On February 7th, I visited Rose Community Foundation and then each of my previous day jobs in Denver, one after the other in reverse order until I stood before the building of my first day job when I'd arrived in Denver. I thanked them all for everything they'd done for me, and I said goodbye to them.

I was no longer fettered by a nine-to-five schedule. I could write as much as I wanted, every hour of every day in pursuit of The Dream, rather than just the hours I could steal here and there. Everything was going to get better now.

One month later, I got the report that *The Wishing World* had not sold to expectation.

There were no royalties forthcoming, and Tor didn't want *The Wishing World II*. There would be no advance.

It was March of 2017, and my entire plan was shattered.

19

SAY YES TO EVERYTHING

I THOUGHT IT WAS BAD BEFORE when I was standing at the end of my ADA job and contemplating jumping off the cliff, but that was nothing compared to this. Before, I could still run the other direction, back to the safe arms of a reliable career.

Now, I was in the soup. Going back would be almost as much effort as going forward. Not only had I quit my nonprofit fundraising career track, but I'd ramped down for two and a half years as an Executive Assistant. I was three years cold to the industry, three years away from being a useful, marketable fundraising professional. I'd blown through a third of my savings already, *The Wishing World* book sales had yielded me zero royalties, and there wasn't another advance coming.

Even if I had another book ready to shop around—which I didn't—it would take about two years for any royalties to follow, if they ever followed. Would any big publisher take a chance on a two-time loser? I'll quote Wreck-It Ralph here:

"To that I say, 'HA!' And… no."

Even if by some miracle I could get another trad publisher to sign me after two proven failures, the advance was going to be minuscule.

There was no help there. I needed money, and it needed to show up in less than eight months.

I threw my frustration into writing. If I couldn't make money, I could at least make product. Maybe I was going to fail in this enterprise. Maybe 2018 would dawn with me looking for a new day job. But I knew for a fact that if I got to the end of 2017 with no money and no new books, I would feel absolutely worthless.

The financial pressure mounted as the year went on and I finally sat down with Lara.

"I don't know what to do," I said, feeling like I'd utterly failed her. As I'd laid out my goals for my fledgling writing business in 2016, I'd promised at least a bit of help this year, and a thriving career that could hold up half the finances by the end of 2018.

I had no prospects for either of those promises.

I was worried Lara was going to say something like, "Well, you tried. Why don't you finish out the year and go look for a job."

But my wife is a different breed than that. She just held my hand, waited for me to go through all my gyrations of failure as a provider and a husband, and she said:

"This is the path, love. It's not about the money. It's about following your heart. If it doesn't make money right now, you're going to have to learn how to be okay with that."

Her response just stunned me. Here I was, falling on my sword because I'd failed her, and here she was trying to pick me back up and telling me to trust in myself, in the process, and in the fact that I was on the right path.

"I just don't know what to do," I said.

"Say yes to everything," she said.

"What?"

"If an opportunity comes along, say yes. If it has to do with writing at all, no matter how small, say yes. See what happens. Everything else will work out. You'll see."

"Everything will work out, eh?"

"You'll see."
"Say yes to everything?"
"To everything."

20

SALESMAN

Say yes to everything…

Lara's statement was a lot like that little whisper in my nightmare, the one that told me I could fly if I could just hold myself together. I had no idea how "saying yes to everything" was going to fix my problems. I mean, for cryin' out loud, nobody was asking me any questions! How could I say yes if there were no offers of any kind?

Except there were. My problem wasn't a lack of opportunity, it was lack of vision to *see* the opportunities. Lara's heartfelt statement stayed with me, and I applied it to everything, not just the traditional publishing path.

For years, I'd been a member of the Colorado Authors League (CAL). I'd joined at the suggestion of the president at the time, Denny Dressman, who I'd met through his work as a committee volunteer at the Juvenile Diabetes Research Foundation.

In general, I've always struggled with being a part of clubs. My style had always been a combination of lone wolfing it or gathering together a handful of really close friends. So I joined because Denny asked me to, and because it seemed like something a "real author" would do. Through the years, I would sometimes wonder what use that membership was to me…

But CAL was about to change my career.

CAL sent out periodic newsletters, as every organization has done since the beginning of organizations, and generally I had ignored them. But with my new mantra planted firmly in my mind, and with no direction, I decided one day to poke around in the newsletter for opportunities.

"Come join the CAL holiday booth!" the newsletter said. I reached out to the new president Barb Lundy—Denny had since stepped down—and asked her what the holiday booth was about.

"It's an opportunity to sell your books," she said. "We purchase three 10x10 booths, and then we give each CAL author a 2-hour slot each day. It only costs $50, and you get to sell directly to the public. Would you like to do it?"

Well that sounds absolutely awful, I thought. *I think I'd rather go to the dentist.*

"Yes," I said aloud.

I paid the $50. I ordered books to sell for the big day, but I was not excited. I didn't like the idea at all. I did not see myself as a salesman. I would rather have stayed home and wrote more books.

But the $10,000 I'd saved up from my days at Rose Community Foundation was spent, and cold, hard reality was setting in. I had to come up with $500 in November just to make ends meet. So if I could make even part of that from this freakin' booth, I had to at least try.

Say yes to everything…

So I showed up for my slot on Friday, and I watched all the other authors for how one should go about doing this. Some would just sit there and watch people go by, engage them if they happened to ask a question. Even fewer would try to draw people in, and that just made me cringe.

"Come on over! We got Colorado authors right here!"

"Want a book from a Colorado author? Come on over here!"

"Books books books!"

Every now and then, a customer would wander over, but mostly I watched them put on their "I'm studiously *not* looking at you" face and avoid eye contact.

I can't do that, I thought. *No way can I do that.*

But I'd said yes to this enterprise, and I knew I would hate myself if I didn't give it everything I had. So I put on my best smile and started calling people over in that same obnoxious fashion.

It felt awful.

And it didn't work.

After doing that for the duration of my very first slot—two hours of being an old-time barker and selling zero books—I went home dejected.

"How did it go?" Lara asked.

"Horrible," I said. "I felt like a cheesy used-car salesman. I hated it. I guess I'm just not cut out for in-person sales."

"Well," she said cheerily. "At least you gave it a try."

That was true. At least I'd said yes. I'd fulfilled my contract, and I *had* tried my hardest, putting myself in an uncomfortable position to try to learn something new.

"You going to go back tomorrow?" she asked.

"Of course," I said. "I mean, I said I would do it, and I'll go back. But this time, I'm going to just be myself. I'm not going to try to be someone else. And if that means just sitting there while the two hours float by, then that's what I'll do."

She kissed me. "Excellent."

Saturday dawned, and I returned to the Denver Mart for my second slot. This time, instead of looking at what everyone else was doing, I just sat there and thought about how much I loved my stories. That made me smile, and so I just smiled at people passing. I began to daydream about my next novel, a little social rant about junk food and addiction that had become a chapter and a half. I had no idea what it was going to become later (for the record, it would evolve into the time travel novel *Charlie Fiction*), but it was far more enjoyable than trying to put on someone else's skin to sell books.

During this rather convoluted and detailed daydream, I suddenly felt like I was being watched. I came back from my reverie and noticed a little girl across the aisle staring at *The Wishing World* banner. She had ahold of her mother's hand, who was turned the other direction buying a Christmas wreath. I smiled at her.

Her gaze shot from the banner to my face. She jolted, then spun around and turned her back.

I stifled my laughter, then went back to plotting my novel.

A few minutes later, the little girl stood there again, this time much closer. She'd left her mom and was about eight feet away from the table.

"Hi there," I said. "Do you like stories like that?" I indicated *The Wishing World* banner.

She nodded.

"Do you want me to tell you a little bit about that story?"

She nodded again.

So I did. I told her about Gruffy the Griffon, Pip the Toucan, and Squeak the Mouse, as well as the Water Princess of the Eternal Sea, and fiery little Lorelei.

Her eyes glittered with interest, and my heart leapt. I wasn't much of a salesman…

But I *was* a storyteller.

This was something I understood. I could do this all day long. The little girl ran away to tell her mother and, apparently, her friends, because thirty minutes later, I had a half-dozen girls and boys gathered around my table, and I told them all about *The Wishing World*.

It clicked for me then. I didn't *have* to be a salesman. I just had to be a storyteller. So instead of doing the used-car salesman routine or the "I'm just going to sit here until something happens" routine, I began looking at the people who passed the booth. I watched their eyes, and if their gaze got caught on any of the banners or books on the table, I crafted a question for them.

"Do you like fantasy books?"

I sold nearly twenty copies by the end of the day. By the time the weekend ended, I'd sold 33 total—the most of any single author that weekend. Suddenly, I had authors coming up to me and asking what my secret was.

But there was no secret. I wasn't trying to make a sale at all costs. I wasn't trying to railroad someone into making a purchase they didn't want. I honestly wanted to connect readers to books they would love. I was just telling stories.

That was my job. The CAL holiday booth showed me one thing clearly: there were people out there who wanted my stories. A whole lot of people.

I just had to find them.

21

RAPID RELEASE

IN DECEMBER OF 2017, just after the CAL holiday fair, our family finances were about to collapse.

I was one year in, a point at which I was supposed to have $20K in hand, and I'd made $1,400.

I was right on the edge, but there was a new possibility in the wind. I'd needed $500 for November, and that was almost exactly what I'd made at the CAL holiday booth.

I needed another $500 for December, so I signed up for another holiday booth in Georgetown. I made nearly $300. It wasn't the whole enchilada...

But I felt something new. A possibility. A path forward. A way out of the darkness.

Once, I'd needed to impress an agent, an editor, or a publisher in order to even put my money on the roulette wheel and spin it. Then I'd wait in anticipation that my books would generate interest, make me money. I'd hope that the publisher would get my stories in front of the people who craved them, that I could build an audience.

After the holiday fair, I saw that I could have a direct line to my audience. It wasn't a large audience yet—just thirty-three people, but I'd just cut out all the waiting and all the middle men. I didn't have to ask permission of anyone to get a spin at *this* roulette wheel. I could go to a holiday fair and make hundreds of dollars, and I wasn't waiting on anyone to give me a thumbs up or down; I wasn't reliant on someone who "may not get my story" or who "thought this other author's story would have a better chance at success." I was the captain of this ship.

Granted, hundreds of dollars wasn't a lot—it wasn't the fulfillment of The Dream—but I was in control. I could move the needle single-handedly.

Through events, my income shortfall in December got taken care of. Then Lara got promoted. Her increase in salary bought another two months. Then our income tax return came in. We got another six months.

My writing business had new life, a new time clock had started, and I wasn't about to waste it. I decided to take this new selling-in-person thing for a spin.

I signed up for six selling opportunities in 2018 throughout the year, including the holiday fairs I'd done the previous year.

Now, math is not my specialty. I tend to think in large scope and let the details work themselves out, and math is *all* about the details.

However, I do have access to spreadsheets. I plugged in the numbers and took a look. How much had I earned at the CAL holiday fair? How much had I spent on the booth, gas, food, parking, and of course for the books I'd sold?

I came to a firm conclusion: I couldn't possibly make a living at doing in-person sales. It was a stop-gap at best. Earning a few hundred here and a few hundred there was barely going to cover the expenses it took to do the actual con. Sometimes I might get a hundred or so in net revenue, so I could push our finances a month forward, maybe two, but my real goal was to replace the income I'd been making at the ADA. Or at least replace the income I'd been making at Rose

Community Foundation, which was substantially lower.

In-person sales wasn't going to do that. The most I'd made so far at a single event was around $500, and I could barely imagine making twice that. And if I did that and went to, say, ten selling events in 2018, I'd still only make about $10K for the year, most of which would get eaten up by expenses.

But I had felt the rush of the indie life, that I could do this relatively alone and get the money now. Waiting on the trad publishing industry meant I'd be back at a day job by July.

Also, by 2018, the indie publishing wave was rising. It had moved out of the swampy basement and into the mainstream. Interesting things were happening. There were people who were marrying their fate to Amazon and making fantastic financial strides in their careers. Kindle Unlimited was becoming a thing. E-books were more and more a fact of life, and some of these indie authors were cleaning up by targeting those readers who loved to devour e-book after e-book.

Now to be fair, most people who threw their novels up as an e-book still weren't cracking the code, weren't making more money than me, but there were some business-minded authors who were killing it.

In early 2018, at a conference called Superstars Writing Seminars—which Chris Mandeville introduced me to—I met an indie publisher married team who had just made $90,000 in 2017 rocking the indie method.

And they were willing to talk about their success and how they'd done it.

This was the next phase for me. This was the new version of The Dream. I stalked them, went to their talks, and pulled them aside in the hallway and asked them one-on-one questions, which they generously answered in detail.

Much of what they said about marketing, keywords, advertising, categories, audience targeting, and comps went right over my head, but I scribbled notes as fast as I could.

When I returned home, I got to work researching these things. I'd also discovered 20BooksTo50K, which was an organization founded by an author named Michael Anderle and championed by an author named Craig Martelle.

Back when I was struggling to let go of my day job, Michael Anderle was looking at the trends of e-book publishing. He had released a book, then another, then a third, and he studied the income. For each book he was making a few dollars a day. He did the math and realized that if he could publish 20 books, he could make $50K over the course of a year. And if he did that, he could let go of his day job, move to Mexico, and live the life of his heart.

By the time I discovered this group, Michael had sailed past his $50K/year goal and was making hundreds of thousands of dollars a year.

I pulled up the 20Books Facebook group and began reading the FAQ page, reading the success stories. It heartened me, and I just knew I could do this.

There were many tips and tricks offered up by the group, but the one I fixated on was rapid release. There was a group of authors who posited that if you could release books rapidly enough, it would capture your audience and make them crave more. That way, you could build an audience quickly.

Perhaps this attracted me because I'd been so frustrated with the slow release policy of trad publishing. These authors were talking about releasing a book every other month. Some were talking about once a month. Some were even talking about releasing a book every three weeks!

I harbored the belief—and still do—that if I could just get people reading my stories, they would love them and carry the baton forward for me. While I couldn't imagine myself writing even a book every other month—let alone every three weeks— I had the *Threadweavers* trilogy in its rough draft form, just waiting to make its debut into the world.

My plan formed.

If I could get all of those books ready, if I could save them up, then I could release them bam-bam-bam, one a month for three months in a row. Then I could realize this rapid release dream and finally kickstart my career.

So I got them all finished, edited, and lined up. I released them one after the other. May, June, July….

It was a glorious, heady time, watching this story of my heart—my beloved first finished series—march out into the world. I waited for the money to roll in, for my audience to form.

It didn't work.

22

THE TWO JOURNEYS

I THINK IT'S IMPORTANT TO POINT OUT a particular aspect about my writer's path. There were two journeys here, running concurrently.

In my life at large there were more, of course. I had a multitude of journeys all meandering side-by-side: my journey as a partner and husband, my journey as a father and mentor, my journey as a friend and comrade amongst my peer group. And many more of lesser importance than those.

But for the purposes of this book, let's just talk about the two journeys that had to do with writing: The business journey and the craft journey.

While I was banging into the walls of professional publishing—trad and indie—worrying about finances, trying to grow my credibility and my audience, I had a very different journey going on when it came to building my skill as a writer and storyteller.

I think it's important to put things in context. I'd first dipped my toe into the business world of writing when I was thirty, then I'd retreated. I'd returned at thirty-three, chipping half-heartedly at trad publishing, waiting to be discovered. By the time I polished and released the *Threadweavers* series, I'd only been a full-time student of indie publishing for about four months.

This was not true of my craft journey.

I had now been writing stories for thirty years. If I had an elementary school level of education in the indie publishing business, then my education in the craft of writing was closer to a master's degree.

I hadn't actually received a college degree in writing, but even when I was in college, I believed that institutions of higher learning could only teach me so much about writing, because what they taught was only a certain flavor. According to the teachers of creative writing at my college, genre fiction was not "real fiction." So there was only so much academia was going to benefit the kind of writing I wanted to do.

To this day, I maintain that the best way to learn writing— to be cutting edge at it—is to write. Every day. Schooling can bolster some skills, can help a writer jump over early pitfalls and fatal flaws in a story, but school will also teach from its engrained perspective on literature.

These days, the publishing industry is moving and evolving daily. Technology continues to update. The way readers access stories continues to update. Readers' tastes change. Genres split and compound and expand and transform all the time.

Did we have a dinosaurs-and-cowboys genre when I was a kid? Did we have game-lit harem novels? LitRPG? Military SciFi?

No. No, we did not.

To keep up with reader interest and demand, to understand today's writing and market, the best and swiftest way is to step out of the classroom and into the raging river itself.

Write your books, then test them by putting them into the world. And the cool thing is: writers can do this with relative ease. As I mentioned before, it is shamefully easy to publish your stories.

The highest-level author skills are found by simply writing, writing, and writing more. Even academics would agree that the trickiest thing for a writer to master is voice, and the only way to find your voice is to spend time with yourself, writing.

This was what I had been doing. Writing, writing, and more writing. This was my default mode when I got scared of the publishing industry. It became my primary focus once I realized I could build my own audience. I no longer had to wait for trad publishing to make moves on my behalf. Now I had direct access to my audience. The only thing keeping me from selling more books to them was me.

My greatest strength was the education I'd built in writing stories. I had to showcase that. I had to make it even better.

It was time to kick up the level of my production in all the ways.

23

WRITER'S ADRENALINE

SO NOW INDIE PUBLISHING—especially online—was the carrot drawing me forward. I had talked to people who had gone from my position—making less than $10,000 a year—to making over $100,000 a year, but I hadn't been able to duplicate it.

In-person sales was my "I know I can do this, so I'm going to do it" publishing activity. I knew in-person sales was never going to transform into The Dream, but it kept some cash flowing and allowed me to explore new selling opportunities.

I also had to continue improving my writing skills. Deep down, I knew that's where the juice was. You can make all the contacts in the trad publishing world. You can get the top agent, the best editor, the most friendly publisher. You can figure out every trick in indie publishing—advertising, marketing, pricing, blurb writing, rapid release timing—all of it.

But in the end, it's going to come down to the book the writer writes. It's going to come down to those readers who love it. If you have enough readers who love what you do, they're going to tell other people. If you can capture that attention with your craftsmanship, your audience will do the work of making your book immortal. It's the only thing that ever has.

Writing the stories was my passion. It was my strength. It was where the largest portion of my expertise lay, and I loved doing it.

Despite the failures in my trad-business journey and the brick walls I'd slammed into during my fledgling indie journey, I never lost my love of making the stories. I never stopped believing that *this* was my most important talent.

Now, let me give a short recap of the growth of the development of my craft.

When I started writing, I emulated the novels I'd loved as a teenager, and that's pretty much where my mind got stuck for decades. I wanted to do what Weis and Hickman had done. I wanted to do what Terry Brooks and Piers Anthony had done.

During my college days and the decades after, I didn't want anyone to teach me anything about writing. That inclination probably started with my high school English teacher hating my style—and genre—of writing. It continued with some of my literarily-inclined high school friends, who joined their voices to that opinion. It finished with my college professors looking down on genre fiction. All of this made me hide what I was doing.

I didn't want their derisive opinions anywhere near my stuff. I didn't want negative feedback killing the joy of creation. Their voices weren't helpful. I wanted to discover my own voice. I leveraged selective ignorance. I clung to my mantra:

If the feedback is not helping you drive your writing forward, it IS NOT USEFUL.

The walls I put up were beneficial and detrimental. It helped because I got to foster my little characters and worlds without interference. It hurt me because I ignored/overlooked a number of tools that might have helped me advance the art of my craft faster.

Sometimes it isn't the tools themselves that are bad. It's

the timing. Artistic creation is a weird beast, and sometimes it needs to be teased out at the right moment, not a moment before. College was clearly not the moment for some of this advice, at least for me. That is not to say that all that advice was gold and I was blind. Some of it was absolute crap. But some of it was good, and I ignored that too. I threw the baby out with the bathwater because I needed to get my feet underneath me. It was far more important that I keep writing than absorb all the relevant tools at the time.

Only after I had run down some roads into dead-ends, only after I had discovered some secrets on my own did I begin to wonder what secrets I might have overlooked back then, secrets offered by people who'd already walked their own dead-ends.

This was when I finally decided to read *Save the Cat* by Blake Snyder.

Save the Cat is a screenwriting how-to book published by Blake Snyder, who wrote screenplays for big producers and directors in the '80s and '90s (like Stephen Spielberg). I won't toot his horn, as he does quite well on his own in that book, but many of my writing friends had been raving about *Save the Cat* and the Three-Act structure for screenplays for years.

Up until 2019, I had avoided it and all other writing how-to books.

But as I was beginning to pick up momentum in my career, as I felt more and more secure in my voice, I decided I could risk outside input. I mean, if I hated it, I could just throw it away. So I began reading *Save the Cat*.

It took half a chapter to suck me in. I flew through it.

I hadn't realized how hungry I'd become for this. The timing was now right for me. I wanted education now. I soaked it up like a sponge, filling in gaps and advancing my skills at a staggering pace. It was a revelation.

Blake Snyder turned story inside out and then right side back again. He explored new avenues of genre I'd never heard of before. He distilled successful storytelling into something quantifiable, beat for beat.

He described movies as "emotion-making machines" and said that those who made them were masters at eliciting specific emotions from the audience based on the structure he discussed.

The emotional beats he laid out in his *Save the Cat* beat sheet were similar to what I'd discovered organically myself through a process I call Node Writing, except Blake Snyder put the emotional beats in order, explained them, their purpose, and how to properly leverage them.

After *Save the Cat*, I devoured *Save the Cat Writes a Novel* by Jessica Brody, a remix of the original concept but applied directly to novel writing instead of screenplay writing. That became my true template; I read the first quarter of that book twenty times. I still go back and read it from time to time.

These new tools were like a rush of adrenaline to my writing. I'd never thrown any kind of structure over my writing before, but as I embarked on my next project, *Tower of the Four*, I had two grand intentions.

First, I was going to focus on simplicity. Everything was going to center around four characters and one keep called The Champions Academy. I was going to make a magic system based on the number 4. Emotional, Mental, Spiritual, and Physical magic. One, two, three, four. Simple, right?

Second, I was going to follow the *Save the Cat* methodology and create a beat sheet for the whole thing.

And that's exactly what I did. My craft renaissance started turning heads, and my subsequent work began to grab finalist tags, then finally win awards.

And this, in turn, helped my push on the business side of writing.

24

THE MUSE

2019 SAW *CHARLIE FICTION* BECOME my first award notable, getting a finalist tag from the Colorado Authors League, though it did not win.

However, my efforts to increase my online sales failed. The rapid release of *Threadweavers* had done nothing to elevate me or my works on Amazon's powerhouse marketplace. The huge push to get everything out in 2018 left me thin in the production arena heading into 2019, and I only released one book that year: *The Undying Man*, the long-awaited sequel to *Fairmist*.

However, my in-person sales events over 2019 were interesting. I made it to six events that year, including some big ones like FanX in Salt Lake City, Denver Comic Con, Albuquerque Comic Con, and Santa Fe Comic Con. At two of them, I'd made over $1,000. That was a giddy threshold. I'd never made $1,000 online at Amazon in one month. I'd barely hit $500. Heck, in 2017, I'd earned $1,400 for the whole year, but now I was bringing in nearly that much at just one event.

As encouraging as that was, what I was most excited about

as I headed into 2020 was that the Save-the-Cat generated *Tower of the Four* was done, a 95K-word novel. I did a quick outreach to my old agent, Donald Maass, to see if he and trad publishing might be interested.

I didn't hear back.

I waited a month, then I moved on. I was through spending time on trad publishing, waiting for them to notice me. I had to get things moving now.

Since my big release year in 2018 and its follow-up one-book year, I thought perhaps rapid release hadn't worked for me because I hadn't been able to maintain that pace for more than four months in a row. I'd counted on *Threadweavers* to get readers interested, but it hadn't panned out in that short, three-month span. What if I needed to keep up that pace for an entire year to see positive results?

Well, I knew I couldn't write a 90K-word book every month, so I reworked my thinking. What if I released something every month, but not a full novel?

I decided to break *Tower of the Four* into 30K-word episodes. I was capable of producing 30K words every month. If I could follow through on that, I'd generate three months of releases, then start releasing them while I worked on the next three, then the next three, all the way to the end of the year.

2020 brought another Colorado Authors League finalist tag for *The Undying Man*, but not a win. I kept working.

Tower of the Four, Episode 1: The Quad, came out, and the others followed one after the other. April, May, June. I spent $500 on Amazon advertising to jump start the thing.

I made $365 in return.

The disappointing sales left a bad taste in my mouth, but I pressed on. I'd known that just three months wasn't going to tell the tale, and I worked hard on the next three episodes.

But the best laid plans often get hijacked by my creative mind. As I started working on *Tower of the Four, Episode 4: The Nightmare*, I got side tracked by another idea that had been percolating for years.

I'd had a few adventures in my twenties, hitchhiking across

the country, almost dying several times climbing—in addition to the moment in the oil tanker—and I'd been toying with the idea of writing it all down. I'd been considering this autobiographical book for about thirty years.

So of course in the midst of trying this rapid release strategy, I woke up one morning and tried to write the first chapter of this potentially autobiographical story.

I failed.

But as often happens when I fail, I got stubborn. I woke up the next morning, scrapped the original chapter, and wrote a brand new chapter 1.

It sucked.

I went to sleep, woke up the next morning, scrapped the second chapter 1, and tried again.

This time I kind of liked it. I wrote chapter two. I liked that one as well. I wrote chapter three.

Now, I am an inspirational writer. I love the rush of euphoria when I get into a groove. Hours can seem like minutes when the muse stands at my shoulder, whispering in my ear.

However, I have trained myself to write regardless. If the muse chooses not to visit, I will gut it out anyway, get in my words, push my way through. I have found that if I just get myself started, she almost always arrives shortly after. I believe firmly in the saying:

"The muse will find you, but she has to find you working."

Inspiration is often kick-started by hard work. There are moments when the rush of inspiration will carry me forward, but I've also found that if I wait for inspiration to strike, I write far less than I otherwise would.

The story changed. This autobiography slowly slid into fiction, and I began to write what would later be called *Summer of the Fetch*. As I released the notion of it being an accurate-to-life story, I felt the muse draw near.

I had felt the touch of the muse before. I felt it in college when I wrote *Wildmane*. I felt it when I was charting the wet wilds of *Fairmist*. I felt it when I was jumping all around in my crazy Node Writing experiment with *Charlie Fiction*. I'd felt it to a greater or lesser degree in every single novel I'd ever written.

I'd never felt anything like this.

I remember writing the final chapter 1 of *Summer of the Fetch*—my third attempt at starting the story. I remember writing chapter 2, and chapter 3…

I don't remember anything specific after that, not where I was or even really what day it was. The narrative rushed through me. It was like the story was a reservoir of water that had been waiting behind a dam for thirty years. Once the gate opened, the story came on like a flood.

Of course, I didn't want it to stop. This was what you hear about, what you read about, what authors try to describe when they get taken by a passion.

During the first four days of this ridiculous writing jag, I felt like the luckiest person in the world. I didn't really have to make any decisions; I just had to keep my fingers flying over the keyboard. Over the course of the following four days, I could barely believe it. I mean, I'd had spurts of inspiration before, but never for more than a couple of days. This eight-day, unceasing, unstoppable gush of creativity was… well, I didn't even *know* what it was, but I wasn't about to quit.

As I crested the tenth day, my joy changed to pain. The flood of inspiration wouldn't stop, and it hurt. My ass was sore from sitting in the chair twelve hours a day. My brain was fatigued, not just from lack of sleep, but from constant use, sorting plot lines, envisioning and holding together character arcs, capturing the descriptions of a road trip across the western United States.

But I could feel it all building. I could feel it all coming together, and I couldn't stop now. What if I stopped and the muse left? What if I got three-quarters of the way through the book, decided to take a break, then came back to find that it was all gone?

That terrified me. I stayed on the wave. I didn't care about sleep. I forgot to eat.

My kids and my wife stayed far back during this process, at

least up to the eleventh day. They knew I was in the throes of creation. I'd snapped at each one of them before when they'd bothered me in this state. They knew the signs, but it had never gone on this long, not even half this long.

Sometime on the eleventh day, Lara came into my office. She held a plate with steaming grilled chicken, broccoli, and rice.

"You need to eat," she said softly. "Do you want to eat?"

"Yes," I said. "Yes, please. Thank you so much." I practically cried then. I wanted to stop. I wanted to tell her that I wanted to come downstairs and play board games with them, watch a movie. I wanted to do anything other than stay a slave to this flood that absolutely would not stop.

But I didn't dare.

I thanked her about a dozen times in the two minutes that I turned my attention to her.

"You sure you don't want to take a break?" she asked.

"I do," I said. "But I can't."

She looked like she was considering *making* me take a break, then thought better of it.

"I'll be done soon," I said. "I just can't… I can't…"

I never finished that sentence. I turned back to the story and jumped in. I don't know how long Lara stood there. It could have been another thirty seconds. It could have been another thirty minutes.

I don't remember eating the food.

Two days later, I finished the novel.

And I loved it. I loved it so much. My heart spilled over with joy.

I was hungry. I was exhausted. I wanted to see the sun. But I securely saved the document in Scrivener, exported the file to Word, and emailed a copy to myself and to Lara for safekeeping.

Then the rush left me. I imagined the muse blowing me a kiss from the corner of my room and vanishing. With her went all of my energy. I staggered from my desk to my bedroom and slept for two days.

When I awoke, I was afraid to see what I'd written. I'd had so little control over any of it. The story was alive in my mind, this beautiful little gem that I'd now have forever, but I had no idea if what I saw in my mind was actually on the page.

This gloriously painful process had hijacked my *Tower of the Four* rapid release plan. I had specific intentions for my production in 2020, but apparently the muse had had other plans.

As it turned out, the world had also had other plans. For all of us.

In February, Covid 19 hit the States.

Caught between the growing hysteria about Covid, the hijacking of the muse, and the uncertainty of the future, my plan for rapid-releasing *Tower of the Four* crumbled away.

I barely noticed. I had experienced yet another threshold with writing, and I suddenly saw that there were many more, maybe an infinite number of them. I'd graduated from journeyman to professional writer. I knew what I could do, and I was learning secrets about story that most writers never uncover. The muse had flowed through me, had practically taken over my body. Yet, as miraculous as that was, it only showed me how much further there was to go. I suddenly knew, with unbridled excitement, that there was so much more to learn.

The next step had started to form.

25

ALIGNING FOR SUCCESS

AFTER *SUMMER OF THE FETCH*, my perception about my writing and my career changed. Yes, I still wanted The Dream. I still wanted the money. I wanted the appreciation and the accolades, but the muse's visit had thrown me into a state.

More than the money, more than The Dream that had pulled me forward for so long, I wanted to produce amazing, timeless stories. I wanted to dance with the muse, to be worthy of that feeling. And if that meant I couldn't do it fast, I didn't care, even if it meant I missed out on the rapid-release payoff.

What I'd felt when making *Summer of the Fetch*... I wanted to give that to my readers.

In another time, in another life, when I'd been in my early twenties, I'd promised my best friend that I'd go looking for magic with him, and we'd finished that adventure lost, unsure, and without the goal we'd set out to attain: proof of magic.

Yet here, after thirty years, right in my office, I'd just felt it. I'd been overtaken by a relentless power. This visit from the muse, the fetch, the Universe, or whatever you wanted to call it, had been real.

And I had the manuscript to prove it.

I worked my ass off revising *Summer of the Fetch* and writing the next *Tower of the Four* episodes right up to the first week of July, when another opportunity popped up for me that was not to be missed.

Through a series of circumstances, my 14-year-old son and I embarked on a 5-week, 450-mile trek from Denver to Durango through the Rocky Mountains on the Colorado Trail.

The entire story is chronicled in my memoir *Ordinary Magic*—a title that was no doubt a subconscious extension of what I was feeling at the time. I won't repeat that particular journey here, but you can read about it in the book—or listen to in my voice if you prefer audiobooks.

The hike with Dash took me through the summer. I finished up two more *Tower of the Four* episodes before the end of the year, and entered 2021 with decisions to be made.

As you might imagine, The Year of Covid was a bad year for in-person sales. Everything had shut down. The only event I got to do that year was Albuquerque Comic Con, and only because it was in January before the U.S. was aware of Covid.

In 2021, however, everything started opening up again. And then closing again. And then opening. And then closing. There were waves of "It's safe to go out again! Oh wait, no it's not! Oh wait, yes it is! No, it's not!", but I could ride those waves. I went to the events that were open, and I saw revenue increases in each of them. As the country rose out of Covid permanently, I was excited to see just how much I could make at a con.

The world was getting back on its feet, and success was about to pay me a visit.

26

THE GOOD REVIEWS

LET'S TALK ABOUT SUCCESS.

If you've stuck with me this far, you've seen how many times I've run at a hill only to tumble back down, how many times I've tried for open doors only to have them slammed in my face.

2021 opened up with success on several fronts.

I'd submitted *Tower of the Four: The Champions Academy*, an omnibus volume combining Episodes 1-3, to both the CAL Awards and the Colorado Book Awards, which was run by the state.

I'd submitted to both before, and while I'd made the finalist round a couple of times with CAL, I'd never made the finalist round for the Colorado Book Awards before.

Tower of the Four did. Not only did I gather my first finalist tag for the Colorado Book Awards for *Tower of the Four*, but I got my first win from the Colorado Authors League. *Tower of the Four: The Champions Academy* took the epic fantasy category, and *Summer of the Fetch* got a finalist tag for the young adult category.

I was ecstatic.

This was the beginning of The Dream, right? Accolades from the writing community. I rode the high, feeling validated. I'd been trying for years to win the CAL Award, and to be mentioned in the Colorado Book Awards. Now I had both.

In addition, my reputation as an epic fantasy author and my connections with other writers in the community had got me an invitation to do book bundles and anthologies with big names like Jim Butcher, Kevin J. Anderson, and Craig Martelle.

To pile on the good news, I'd recently been invited to become a partner in a new multi-author, shared-world, mega-epic fantasy project called *Eldros Legacy*. The original founders were Rob Howell, Marie Whittaker, Mark Stallings, and Quincy J. Allen. And they wanted a fifth.

It was Mark Stallings who reached out to me and, after an hour-long conversation, I agreed to do it.

It was perfect timing. After years of working on my own, I was actually in the mood for a collaboration. I'd started something earlier that year that went nowhere because of creative differences—everyone wanted to do a different genre and the resulting project was a muddle at best.

But *Eldros Legacy* was pure, unadulterated epic fantasy. Just my cup of Chai. Not only that, but we had the nod from Chris Kennedy Publishing (CKP), who had agreed to publish us. CKP was experienced with a very successful multi-author military sci-fi world called *The Four Horsemen*, and they wanted to repeat the success in the epic fantasy genre. I dove in headfirst.

This was the beginning of *Khyven the Unkillable*.

I wanted to do my best. I wanted to impress my new colleagues and my new publisher, so I set to work right away. The group had all collectively agreed to put out one book a month starting in December. Between the founders, at least five other cohort authors (writers who were invited to write in the world, but weren't founders), and two Eldros short story anthologies, we planned to release one book every month in 2022.

This was an answer to the nearly overwhelming rapid-release theory. Maybe I couldn't release a book a month by myself, but with a dozen of us working on *Eldros Legacy*, surely we could…

My manuscript wasn't due until November at the earliest, but I worked with a fervor in February, leveraging my newfound love for the structure of *Save the Cat*. I repeated my process—such that I ever repeat any process with a book—from *Tower of the Four*. I looked for the beats. I paced the novel. I heightened the emotional tension points for the reader.

I finished *Khyven the Unkillable* a couple months before the accolades from CAL and the Colorado Book Awards started rolling in for *Tower of the Four* and *Summer of the Fetch*.

Not only that, but the insider feedback started coming back on *Khyven the Unkillable*, and it was glowing. They loved it. I had finalist tags and awards for my most recent books. Fantastic excitement and insider buzz about *Khyven the Unkillable*.

I felt invincible.

Failure is hard, but they say success can be more dangerous. I'd never bought into that bit of wisdom. That seemed silly. I'd always welcomed whatever success came my way, but as I passed that summer and moved into the fall, I ran into a problem.

I'd finished *Khyven the Unkillable* six months ahead of schedule, but I was about two years behind on finishing the third and final installment of *The Whisper Prince* trilogy, *The Slate Wizards*.

Once I finished *Khyven*, I hunkered down to write *The Slate Wizards*…

It was arduous, the opposite of what I'd experienced with *Summer of the Fetch*. From chapter one, I struggled. I pushed and pushed until I had 50K words, then I gave up with a gasp.

I simply couldn't force myself forward anymore. The muse was nowhere to be found. It was as though she had sucked all the creative wind from my sails. I kept second-guessing myself. I even used the *Save the Cat* structure, but I kept changing my mind, rearranging things, grinding to a halt.

With horror, I realized I had writer's block for the first time. Up to that point, I'd always prided myself that writer's block was for other writers. I could always pivot. I could always skip to a part of the story I was inspired to write.

But I'd tried that, and every time I came to a dead-end.

I felt caged. *This* was the book I needed to write to finish out the trilogy. Fans were waiting for *this* novel. I couldn't just go write another novel, but I simply could not make myself push forward any further.

After a month of no writing, where I struggled to understand what was happening to me, I finally realized what it was, what was stopping me, why I was second-guessing myself and failing to get into the groove.

I'd bought into the hype about my own books.

It took me a while to untangle that from my emotional mess, but essentially it was this:

I'd forgotten Margaret Weis's advice: "You can't listen to the bad reviews, but you can't listen to the good reviews, either."

I'd let the good reviews get to me, the awards and finalist tags, the rave comments about *Khyven the Unkillable*. The demons whispered insidious questions in my ear, like:

What if The Slate Wizards *is worse than your last two books? What if you're going backward? What if it isn't an award-winner-in-the-making? What if you've lost your mojo…?*

I suddenly realized the demons had been chewing on me for months, and I hadn't even noticed.

The Little Rebel had been silent for a good long while, and I think he finally tired of my emotional game of Twister.

"Fuck this," the Little Rebel said. "If that book don't wanna be written, screw it. Write another book."

More frightened than anything else, I cast *The Slate Wizards* aside and gave myself a break through the holidays. I didn't think about it. I tried to clear my mind.

When 2022 rolled around, I reset. I told myself to write a crappy novel—my favorite advice to new novelists. I told myself to shake off the restraints of my own new expectations. The phrase "write a crappy novel" is something I use all the time when I'm teaching writing courses, or just giving hallway advice at a conference. As I mentioned before, I think the greatest threat to young writers—and clearly sometimes veteran writers—is not finishing their novels. That stems from low confidence.

I'd lost my confidence during the beginning of *The Slate Wizards*, and the Little Rebel was right. I had to move on. I had to run the other direction. *The Slate Wizards* was simply too rife with emotional pitfalls to return to it right away.

I pivoted. I threw my efforts into *Lorelle of the Dark*, the second in my *Eldros Legacy* series. I told myself it didn't have to be great. I told myself if I wrote it far enough ahead of schedule, and it sucked, I would have plenty of time to edit it before it was due. I told myself my Eldros comrades would forgive me if book 2 was a sophomore slump.

I told myself anything and everything to get me started.

I wrote *Lorelle* in two months. It was good. Some of my confidence returned, and I immediately began writing the third book, *Rhenn the Traveler*. I was back in the groove. I breathed a huge sigh of relief.

I learned a big lesson on that one, and it was two-fold. First, I couldn't get too wrapped up in my own hype. Never ever. I now saw clearly how good reviews might trip me up as surely as the bad. The bad reviews created a lack self-confidence. But the good reviews created a lack of self-confidence on the flip side of the coin. The former made me doubt I could write a good book. The latter made me doubt I could write a *better* book.

Eventually I returned to center. Don't listen to the bad reviews. Don't listen to the good.

Create the books that wanted to come forth. Let the readers decide with their interest and with their money if they were good or bad. It wasn't my job to determine what my manuscripts were beforehand. My job was…

To write.

27

BEGINNER'S MIND

I'D BEEN CROSSING TUMULTUOUS THRESHOLDS within my journey in the craft of writing, but let's turn back to the journey of the business of writing. At the dojang where I trained and received my 2nd Dan black belt in Taekwondo, we have a list of things to remember. They are posted on the wall. These are the four basic tenets to strive toward when you enter the dojang:

1. Set a goal
2. Give 100%
3. Positive Attitude
4. Beginner's Mind

This chapter will be focused on the last one.

Beginner's Mind means that, in order to be successful in your training, you must be receptive to that training, no matter how much you've learned or how far you've come down the path. Even the most accomplished black belts still have something to learn, and retaining a Beginner's Mind opens you up to improve your skills, no matter how formidable those skills might already be.

Let's apply it to selling events.

By 2021, I'd been building my success at selling events for years. It had started as a "just say yes to everything" exercise. It had become a "This is better than nothing, but I'm never going to make a living with it."

In the fall of 2021, I was about to have a revelation. My perspective on comic cons was about to change.

First, though, I was going to get a big fat reminder of Beginner's Mind.

I had been building a reputation. Among my peers, I was one of the best at con selling. Back in 2018, I wondered if I could even hit $1,000 at a con. By September of 2021, I had exceeded the $2,000 level twice. So when I rolled into FanX Salt Lake City that year, I was feeling pretty confident about my hand-selling skills.

Up to this moment, my main goal at a con was to meet fans, convert readers into fans, and get more books out into the world. If I could take home a few dollars above the money it took to pay for the con, I was happy.

But I started to think… if I could make $2,000, why not $3,000? And if $3,000, why not $4,000? Why not $5,000? After some quick calculations concerning set expenses (like booth costs, which stays relatively the same) and flexible expenses (like book costs, which increase the more books I sell), I realized that after about the $3,000 threshold, the income started to leave the set expenses behind.

As I sat behind my booth at FanX, waiting for the first attendees to come through the door, I passed these numbers through my head, double checking them on my calculator. I suddenly realized that the in-person sales events—which I'd always thought of as a financial dead-end—might be the opposite. I might be able to reach that mythical $50K/year through this very avenue.

With a little internal whoop of excitement, I set about tackling the first day of FanX. I was gonna sell Sell SELL!

Now, coming off my recent $2K victory in Colorado Springs and my encouraging math, I was feeling cocky about my selling ability. I felt like I was at the top of my game. I had set up my little 6-foot booth and was ready to kill it.

And I proceeded to watch the author across the aisle from me put my sales to shame.

My arrogance faded as I watched him reel in customer after customer like an expert fisherman, casting his line out and bringing it back in. My arrogance popped like the bubble it is, and I felt miserable as he succeeded again and again as I tried to hook people and failed.

With my ego in tatters, I approached him when the day was done. I introduced myself, and he told me his name was Lance Conrad. I told him that I'd seen his amazing selling ability throughout the day, and we got to talking. I asked him how much he'd sold that day. He said, "66."

I was floored. I'd sold 14.

I picked my jaw up off the floor, swallowed my pride, and asked him, "How do you do it?"

I didn't expect him to answer. I honestly didn't think he would, but he went through his process step by step.

"It starts with the Hook," he said. The Hook is the phrase that pulls people over to the booth. It's not the pitch. The pitch is the compelling mini-story you tell them after you've got their attention. It's the closing argument, but the Hook gets them to listen in the first place.

After we talked about the Hook, he went into the pitch, recommending that I make mine as short and compelling as possible. "Let me hear it."

I pitched him.

"I like that," he said. "It's exciting. You definitely have a flair for storytelling, but it's too long. I'd shorten it down to thirty seconds if you can, sixty seconds if you can't make it that short."

That very night at my friend Aaron's house, even after a long day of selling, I reworked my pitch and got one of his children to listen to it. They helped me shape it up, and the next day I went back to the con prepared to give it a whirl.

I sold 77 books that day.

Afterwards, I caught up with Lance and thanked him.

"How'd you do?" he asked.

"77," I said, beaming.

"Hey!" he said, genuinely surprised. "That's fantastic. You know, I've given that advice to a number of writers, but nobody's ever been able to put it to use. Congratulations!"

"Thanks! How'd you do?"

"89."

I laughed. "Well, I guess I've still got my work cut out for me."

"You're going to keep me on my toes," he said.

"I will if I can."

We shook hands and parted ways.

Beginner's Mind. I was grateful I had approached him, tried to learn from him, rather than just silently resenting him for being better than I was.

I tried to drill that into my brain, right then, right there. There's never a "top of the mountain." There's only the top of *this* mountain, then you'd best start looking for the next peak. I told myself never to rest on my laurels, to always try my best, remembering to look around and learn, remembering to keep that Beginner's Mind.

28

LEVELING UP

THAT YEAR AT FANX delivered a quantum leap in my selling skills. It cracked open a door past which I could see a new possibility.

Up to that point, I'd gone through several cycles, trying to make my writing career financially viable. I'd relied on a trad publishing machine that had dropped me twice. I'd wallowed in the despondency of the great publishing mystery: how do I become a beloved author read by millions instead of a guy just writing books alone in his room? I'd danced with skittish desperation, saying yes to everything and hoping to strike on something that worked. I'd twisted myself into knots trying to emulate indie masters: deciphering Amazon algorithms, advertising, rapid release…

Only now did I see a real path forward, a path I could understand, a path I was good at, a path I could implement successfully. The Dream, which had always hovered just out of reach, might not be far away.

I had already turned my eye to every opportunity to evolve my in-person sales, visual and verbal. I'd watched how other people built their booths, sold their wares. I'd taken advice from my stepbrother Sean, who owned a sign shop and made presentations for corporate trade shows and the like, about how to level-up my visual presentation.

It was my con revelation that became the proverbial carrot driving me forward now. I could make a living at this if I could just exceed $4,000 per con. $5,000 would be even better. Cons could be my path to making a living as a writer if I could "go big enough."

I slid into the holidays and went to the Denver Christmas Market, which was where CAL always had their holiday booth. Instead of the $50 slot through CAL, I bought my own booth. The price of entry was a staggering $1200, more money for just the booth than my highest grossing con two years ago.

I took the risk. I put the money down, and that event paid for itself and then some.

I felt a giddy excitement as I finished out the year. There had been no windfall. No angel had descended from on high and offered me a six-figure deal, but I'd made $27,000. From *my* writing.

I could sink my teeth into that. I could work with that. This was what I'd wanted back in 2018, and it had taken four more years to get to this point. Selling at cons wasn't going to put me in a mansion anytime soon, but there were no gatekeepers in my way. There was no waiting. Surpassing that $27K mark was up to me.

I got to work planning it out, putting together a 2023 strategic plan. I set a goal of hitting eighteen selling events.

2023 arrived, and in addition to my con successes, I was on a writing roll. I felt a rhythm between writing and selling/marketing. I finished *Rhenn the Traveler*, the third in my *Eldros Legacy: Legacy of Shadows* storyline, published it, and got straight to work on *Slayter and the Dragon*.

I had a slate of comic cons lined up to hit my goal. Albuquerque Comic Con came first, then Genghis Con, then many others. I pulled out all the stops, pushing myself into 80-hour work weeks between writing, setting up cons, and selling.

But despite the hours, I loved it. I was literally living that ages-old adage:

"Find a job you love, and you'll never work a day in your life."

The only limiting factor was me. I only had so much bandwidth, and I was about to get some help that would make all the difference, a game changer.

It started in 2022. A young writer named Becca Gardner attended Superstars Writing Seminars (SSWS) and started down a path that would soon intersect with my own. By her own admission, she was an extreme introvert, and it was a herculean task for her to attend that conference, far out of her comfort zone. She spent most of that 2022 SSWS helping in the bookstore, standing against the wall, watching the goings-on, and crying in her room whenever the overload of social stimuli became too much for her.

But one thing she did at the conference was meet Rob Howell, a founder of *Eldros Legacy* who was recruiting writers for his continent. He spotted her talent instantly and invited her to submit a piece of writing for *Eldros Legacy*, recommending that she first read a few of the books in the series. She began reading *Khyven the Unkillable*.

She loved it, and not long after SSWS, she messaged me on Facebook and asked if she could write on the continent of Noksonon instead of on Rob's continent.

I said, "Rob recruited you. You'll have to ask him. If he's cool with it, then we can start an audition process for Noksonon."

She asked him. He was okay with it, so Becca and I set up a phone call. The conversation turned into two, then three, then into an ongoing check-in where we would discuss *Eldros*, life, the Universe, and everything.

By the summer of 2022, we were fast friends, and she asked if she could help me with some social media tasks. She killed it. By the end of 2022, I hired her as my virtual assistant.

I'd never had an assistant before, and good grief, I didn't know what I was missing. Becca was marvelous. She not only took the load off me in things that I'm not naturally good at—like social media—but she anticipated other things that might be worthy of my attention.

By the time 2023 rolled around, when I was stretched thin with all the writing and the cons, she avidly looked for new opportunities for me and my brand. When everyone told me it would take years to wedge my way into San Diego Comic-con International, Becca said, "Let me see what I can do, boss."

She got me a table within a month.

We became the team supreme, and she helped me lay out the entire year of cons:

Albuquerque Comic Con, Genghis Con, Planet Comicon, Gary Con, Wicked West Comic Con, Grand Comic Fest, Oddity & Bizarre Expo, FanExpo Denver, San Diego Comic-Con, Colorado Springs Comic Con, FanX, Animate!, Oddity & Fear Fest, Denver Christmas Market, Colorado Country Christmas Gift Show, Dragon Steel, GalactiCon, L.A. Comicon, and the Bighorn Book Nook.

With Becca's help, I not only wrote two books in 2023, but attended 21 cons, exceeding my goal of 18.

Things were falling into place. I had a direction. I had a rhythm, and I suddenly had someone who could help me push the business further and faster than I could alone.

With Becca's help, things started to pop. Every con was an increase over the last. We zoomed past the $4K mark in Kansas City, Denver, and Salt Lake City.

Not only that, but word was getting around that I was an expert in hand selling. I was asked to speak at Superstars Writing Seminars, and then at the 20BooksTo50K Las Vegas conference in November.

That entire holiday stretch was absolutely packed. From the beginning of November to the second week in December, I spent thirty-two out of thirty-eight days at a selling event or traveling to one.

But at the end of the year, victory.

In 2022, I'd made $27,000. In 2023, $47,000.

The plan had worked.

As I relaxed into the holidays—with Christmas parties among lovely friends, holiday foods, and that festive feel that only comes around once a year—I reflected on something another fantastic and successful indie author, Katie Cross, had said to the Eldros Legacy founders:

"Making your career as an indie author is like hacking your way through the jungle. You can pick up skills from other people. You can even follow a path that someone else has made, at least for a while, but in the end, your path is going to be different than any other author. We each have different skills and talents, and we're each going to see—and lean toward—different opportunities. At some point, you're going to have to chop your own way through the jungle. In fact, that may be the *only* way to indie success."

After my gauntlet of selling events, as I relaxed into the holidays, into the embrace of friends and family, I realized that's exactly what I'd done. I'd hacked my way through the jungle. It wasn't a path anyone else had taken, and it was customized to my specific skills.

Every day was a new adventure, and though I was happy to be taking a rest...

I also couldn't wait to get back to it. In fact, I'm going to do that very soon, which means setting this narrative aside. My tale, this book, is about to come to an end.

Before I make my exit, though, I wanted to talk about one more thing...

29

FLYING

WHAT MAKES A GREAT WRITING CAREER?

Is The Dream dead? In this wild west era of the publishing industry, have we moved into territory where it is simply impossible to stand out from the crowd? Is it still possible for you to make a great career?

I don't have a direct answer for you. I don't think anyone does. I suspect it's something only *you* can know. With this book, I've done my best to show you what I did, to let you pick through my failures and successes, to make your own decisions about where you can go next.

For me, a satisfying career has always started and ended with the reason I got into this crazy business in the first place.

The writing. The story.

In the long run, this crazy journey can't be about anything else but service to the story. The pull of story is what gets me up in the morning. The chance to create wonder and inspiration is what pushes me through the mind-flaying, soul-cracking parts of writing, the hardest job I've ever known. I've worked in the shadows for most of my writing career, but as I continue to push, the joy always rises in the most unexpected of places.

I did my first-ever panel at Planet Comicon this year. My assistant and I came up with five options for panels for the organizers at Planet Comicon to choose from: four that I knew I could do well, and one we threw in for pizzazz—that I'd never done before—and that I never expected them to pick.

They chose that one. Of course they did. It was titled *D&D: Storytelling Tips and Tricks from Author Todd Fahnestock.*

Now, I'm a D&D player of old. Really old. I had the original basic box set with the dragon coming out of the water, the spearman with the wooden shield, and the sorceress with the green ball of magic. I even have a T-shirt with that exact picture (if you've seen me at a con, you've seen it). In short, I played religiously back then.

I have played *not at all* lately.

So when that panel got chosen, I was terrified.

"What if they ask me about the rules of 8th edition? Or about, like, cantrip limitations? What if someone wants to discuss mixed class vs. race vs. deified, amplified, calcified modifiers!?! I'm not going to have answers for them!"

"It's about storytelling," Becca told me. "Go tell them about how to make better stories for their role-playing."

So at the last minute, I put together some visuals of good storytelling. Three-Act structure, the Hero's Journey, etc. Y'know, the basics.

We went to Planet Comicon. We rocked the booth on Friday. Then 3 p.m. Saturday rolled around, and a wonderful Planet Comicon volunteer named Bonnie showed up to take me to my panel room. Nervous as I was, I blathered incessantly as we made our way through the crowds.

"You excited?" she asked.

"Oh sure. I mean, I don't think there are going to be more than three people at this panel. I'm not famous or anything. But we're going to have fun."

"You think only three people?"

"Or two. Maybe four. It's fine. This is a new topic for me, so if it's small, that'll be fine. We'll just have a good ole time talking story."

We arrived and...

The room was packed.

I'm not talking about a twelve-seater panel room (I've been to those, too). This was a 270-seater, and it was standing-room only.

I looked at Bonnie, who wasn't bothering to hide a sizeable smirk, then at the identification easel sitting outside the door to make sure this was the right place. It was, indeed, my name on that easel.

"This is me?" I asked, stunned.

"Go get 'em." She waved me in.

Once I got my Powerpoint set up, the microphone adjusted, and my books set up in front of me, I looked out at that huge audience and said:

"So, I was expecting about three people today. I don't know what the rest of you are doing here..."

They laughed. The panel began.

We had an amazing time.

After it was over, back at our booth on the vendor floor, a different volunteer came by and talked to us. He told us they'd had to turn people away from that panel because we'd maxed the room's capacity.

It was the only panel that day where they had to do that.

I've spoken a lot about my difficulties to get where I'm going as a writer, and perhaps I haven't highlighted the successes enough. If that is true, I apologize. I only wanted to illustrate that no matter the challenges, you can push through them. Your creativity, your expression, deserves to be released. The successes are waiting for you, and they are as sweet as you've imagined in your Dream.

Like the reader in Albuquerque who said my books became the bridge between himself and his incarcerated father. They each read one of my books at the same time and then bonded over it when he would visit.

Like the aspiring writer in Denver who told me I'd inspired him to keep pursuing his writing dreams.

Like the eager-eyed cosplayer in Kansas City who told me I, and my stories, were a safe space for them, a place they loved to return to.

Like being invited to writer's conferences as an honored guest.

Like winning awards.

Like hitting a $5,000+ con.

So perhaps I haven't highlighted the joys of these moments enough. Sometimes they're emblazoned across the sky for everyone to see. And sometimes they are internal, rising like the sun in your heart during those quiet moments of reflection when no one else is around.

I love both kinds. How could I not? But even after successes, be they loud or quiet, I still get up every morning. I still dream about story. And I still look forward to the challenges with an eager gleam in my eye, like Khyven entering the Night Ring. I still want to do my best to create that amazing book. I want my own *Dragonlance Chronicles*. My *Shannara* series. My *Ender's Game*.

That great career—whether illustrated by hundreds of people hanging on your next word or from quiet moments of deep satisfaction at your work—starts and ends with the writing: why you do it, how you do it. It starts and ends with what you want to offer the world.

It starts and ends with you.

I'd love to tell you how to do it. I'd love to lay out a map of how to create your phenomenal book. But, of course, having me tell you how to make a great novel is laughable; just as laughable as it is for anyone else to tell you the same. There's no cosmic rubric for this, though a lot of people will try to convince you there is.

Many will tell you they can identify a novel that's *going* to be the next sensation. But if there were people like this, the publishing industry would look completely different. Such a sage would be the golden goose of the industry. If a publishing house had one, they would crank out only books that made millions of dollars.

And they don't.

In short, anyone who tries to convince you they know how to write the next international bestselling novel is either trying to convince themselves of it… or they're about to ask you for money.

These people don't decide what a great novel is. Trad publishing gatekeepers don't. Academic scholars don't. Even seven-figure indie authors don't.

The readers do.

The readers are your ultimate test, and since every single reader is different, it means you have to write *your* story, gather *your* audience.

Just because there is no "cosmically great novel template" is not to say that *I* don't think some novels are better than others. Of course I do. I have my taste just like everybody else, but that's exactly what it is: *my* taste. I don't have a crystal ball—or writerly experience—to determine what story is going to be beloved by the world.

I've read books I thought were absolutely brilliant… and they became the next worldwide sensation. And I've read novels I thought were absolutely garbage… and they *also* become the next worldwide sensation.

Many of my friends vented about how horrible the writing in *50 Shades of Gray* was. I never read that book, but whether I would have loved it or hated it, I'd like to point out that *50 Shades of Gray* went on to make truckloads of cash and, more importantly, to please and entertain millions of readers.

How about J.K. Rowling? I knew so many of my writer friends who cried, "Adverbs are the mark of a bad writer, and have you seen how many adverbs are in those books?"

Yet the *Harry Potter* series was so beloved it defined an era.

And how about *Dune*? Rejected twenty-three times before it finally found a home. Now it's a timeless classic with movies and mini-series trying to capture that story with every new generation.

And, of course, I would be remiss if I didn't throw *Star Wars* into this mix. Right before *Star Wars* first came out, George Lucas's colleagues patted him consolingly on the back because they knew he was finished in the movie industry after spending so much money concocting his ridiculous movie of space ships, ray guns, popsicle light swords, and metal robots that talk. Now *Star Wars* is… Well, it's freakin' *Star Wars*!

Some works of fiction hit like comets, leaving craters in our cultural memory that we still feel today. Was it because their creators wrote the perfect story? No. It was because they believed in their story and found their audience. They held themselves together, and they flew.

You can, too.

Great stories are made great by the readers who love them, not by anyone else. The lucky few writers who find a vast audience will reap vast benefits in return.

And never forget that, right now, we live in a magical age for authors and readers alike. The barriers between readers and storytellers have never been thinner. There is no "mainstream" anymore. The opportunities to connect your story with the readers who will love it are all around you. And if even one of them loves your story so much they overflow with joy, with excitement, with purpose, then your story is great. Celebrate that, then go find more readers just like them.

The Dream isn't dead. It might not look how you thought when you first dreamed it. The Dream might get battered and bent, curved and twisted and transformed, but it is still possible. It always was, and you can have it.

Of course, it's going to take saying yes to everything. It's going to take holding yourself together when you want to come apart. It will undoubtedly take a bit of luck. And it's going to take a metric ton of work.

But you can do it.

Now get out there and fly.

ALSO BY TODD FAHNESTOCK

Eldros Legacy (Legacy of Shadows)

Khyven the Unkillable

Lorelle of the Dark

Rhenn the Traveler

Slayter and the Dragon

Bane of Giants (forthcoming)

Tower of the Four

Episode 1 – The Quad

Episode 2 – The Tower

Episode 3 – The Test

The Champions Academy (Episodes 1-3 compilation)

Episode 4 – The Nightmare

Episode 5 – The Resurrection

Episode 6 – The Reunion

The Dragon's War (Episodes 4-6 compilation)

Threadweavers

Wildmane

The GodSpill

Threads of Amarion

God of Dragons

The Whisper Prince Series

Fairmist

The Undying Man

The Slate Wizards

Standalone Novels

Charlie Fiction

Summer of the Fetch

Non-fiction

Ordinary Magic

Falling to Fly

Tower of the Four Short Stories

"Urchin"

"Royal"

"Princess"

Other Short Stories

Parallel Worlds Anthology — "Threshold"

Dragonlance: The Cataclysm — "Seekers"

Dragonlance: Heroes & Fools — "Songsayer"

Dragonlance: The History of Krynn —

"The Letters of Trayn Minaas"

ABOUT THE AUTHOR

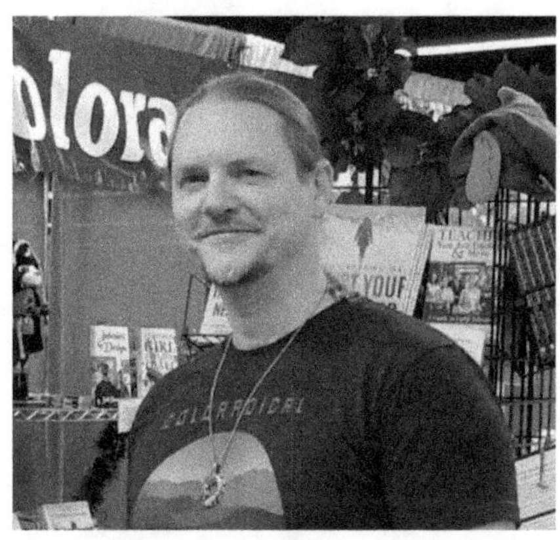

Todd Fahnestock is an award-winning, #1 bestselling author of fantasy for all ages and winner of the New York Public Library's Books for the Teen Age Award. *Threadweavers* and *The Whisper Prince Trilogy* are two of his bestselling epic fantasy series. He is a founder of *Eldros Legacy*—a multi-author, shared-world mega-epic fantasy series—three-time winner of the Colorado Authors League Award for Writing Excellence, and two-time finalist for the Colorado Book Award for *Tower of the Four: The Champions Academy* (2021) and *Khyven the Unkillable* (2022). His passions are great stories and his quirky, fun-loving family. When he's not writing, he travels the country meeting fans, gets inundated with befuddling TikTok videos by his son, plays board games with his wife, plots future stories with his daughter, and plays vigorously with Galahad the Weimaraner. Visit Todd at toddfahnestock.com.

www.ingramcontent.com/pod-product-compliance
Lightning Source LLC
Chambersburg PA
CBHW060635080726
47818CB00004B/149